CHINA
THE LONG MARCH

THE WORLD'S GREAT PHOTOGRAPHERS RETRACE THE ROUTE
ON THE FIFTIETH ANNIVERSARY

LEO MEIER

The publishers would like to thank
the following corporation
who helped to establish this project

Kodak (Export Sales) Ltd

CHINA
THE LONG MARCH

TEXT BY

ANTHONY LAWRENCE

PHOTOGRAPHS BY

BRIAN BRAKE, DI XIANG HUA, KEN DUNCAN, ENRICO FERORELLI,
GEORG GERSTER, GREGORY HEISLER, JEAN-PIERRE LAFFONT, PAUL LAU,
LEONG KA TAI, LIU XIAO JUN, MARY ELLEN MARK, LEO MEIER,
HARALD SUND, HANS VERHUFEN, WANG WEN LAN, ADAM WOOLFITT,
MICHAEL YAMASHITA, YANG SHAOMING, ZHANG HE SONG.

MEREHURST PRESS
LONDON

THE PUBLISHERS THANK THE FOLLOWING
FOR THEIR SUPPORT WITHOUT WHICH
THIS BOOK WOULD NOT HAVE BEEN POSSIBLE:

KODAK (EXPORT SALES) LTD
HUTCHISON WHAMPOA LTD
COOPERS AND LYBRAND
JAMES HARDIE INDUSTRIES LTD
CABLE AND WIRELESS PLC
SHELL CHINA LTD
LAND ROVER LTD
HOLIDAY INN INTERNATIONAL
ASIA/PACIFIC
ANSETT
PANALPINA
HILL AND KNOWLTON

INTERCONTINENTAL PUBLISHING CORPORATION

CHINA NATIONAL PUBLISHING INDUSTRY
TRADING CORPORATION
and
CHINA PHOTOGRAPHIC PUBLISHING HOUSE

Publisher
KEVIN WELDON

Maps
ESTHER LAU
DIANA WELLS

Publishers
LOU MING
WEI LONGQUAN
DENG LIGENG

Project Director
MARY-DAWN EARLEY

Picture Editors
MARY-DAWN EARLEY
ZARA BRIERLEY
CAROLINE ARDEN-CLARKE

Associate Publisher
JOHN OWEN

Advisers
QIN XINGHAN
Director Military Museum
XU XIAOBANG
Director Chinese
Photographers Association

Special Consultants
DR. STEPHEN FITZGERALD
NEIL THOMPSON

Picture Research
KOSIMA WEBER LIU, BEIJING
LAURIE WINFREY, NEW YORK
PAT HODGSON, LONDON & PARIS

Editorial Director
ELAINE RUSSELL

Historical Consultant
WANG HAO

Editors
DEREK A. C. DAVIES
SHEENA COUPE
JACKIE GAFF
FRED ARMENTROUT
HILARY BINKS

Production
SUE TICKNER
LOUISA de BRACKINGHE

Pictorial Consultant
JIANG NINGSHENG

Balloon Pilots
PETER VIZZARD
JUDY LYNNE

Editorial Coordinators
WANG FAYAO
CHEN HONG
LI DONG
QIAO HONG
YANG XIANGXIN

Designer
PETER WONG

Coordinators
CECILLE HAYCOCK
SALLY RODWELL
TERESA ROSE

Design Consultants
EMPHASIS (HONG KONG) LIMITED

PHOTOGRAPHERS

BRIAN BRAKE	NEW ZEALAND	JEAN-PIERRE LAFFONT	FRANCE	HANS VERHUFEN	WEST GERMANY
DI XIANG HUA	CHINA	PAUL LAU	HONG KONG	WANG WEN LAN	CHINA
KEN DUNCAN	AUSTRALIA	LEONG KA TAI	HONG KONG	ADAM WOOLFITT	UK
ENRICO FERORELLI	ITALY	LIU XIAO JUN	CHINA	MICHAEL YAMASHITA	USA
GEORG GERSTER	SWITZERLAND	MARY ELLEN MARK	USA	YANG SHAOMING	CHINA
GREGORY HEISLER	USA	LEO MEIER	SWITZERLAND	ZHANG HE SONG	CHINA
		HARALD SUND	USA		

THIS EDITION PUBLISHED BY:
MEREHURST PRESS
5 Great James Street, London WC1N 3DA

by arrangement with

INTERCONTINENTAL PUBLISHING CORPORATION LTD,

CHINA NATIONAL PUBLISHING INDUSTRY TRADING CORPORATION,

and

CHINA PHOTOGRAPHIC PUBLISHING HOUSE

Typeset in Novarese by Core Bookwork Company, Hong Kong
Colour separations by Universal Colour Scanning Ltd, Hong Kong
Production by Mandarin Offset Pty Ltd
Printed by Toppan Printing Company

ISBN 0 948075 12 0
PRINTED IN HONG KONG
A KEVIN WELDON/CNPITC & CPPH PRODUCTION
FIRST EDITION 1986
REPRINTED 1987

NOTE ON PRONUNCIATION

Chinese names in China: The Long March are spelled according to the Pinyin system,
developed by the Chinese and now generally accepted internationally.
Names written in Pinyin are usually pronounced more or less as written,
but there are some important exceptions:

c	is pronounced as *ts*	(Cao is pronounced *Tsao*)
q	is pronounced as *ch*	(Qing Dynasty is pronounced *Ching Dynasty*)
x	is pronounced as *s*	(Xiang River is pronounced *Siang River*)
z	is pronounced as *dz*	(Mao Zedong is pronounced *Mao Dzedong*)
zh	is pronounced as *j*	(Zhou Enlai is pronounced *Jou Enlai*)

We have not followed Pinyin in cases where an earlier form is so well known that changes
would tend to confuse. We have therefore kept the names of Yangtze River, Sun Yat-sen and Chiang
Kai-shek for the English edition.

LEO MEIER

CONTENTS

INTRODUCTION

THE YEAR 1986 marks the fiftieth anniversary of one of the most momentous events in history: China's Long March, the six thousand-mile retreat of Mao Zedong and his colleagues from the forces of Nationalist general, Chiang Kai-shek — a flight that eventually turned into victory and paved the way for the establishment of Mao Zedong as China's supreme leader for nearly thirty years.

Some eighty-six thousand people, including women and children, began the Long March. They suffered from enemy harassment, malnutrition, disease, frostbite, fatigue (at times despair) and almost every other form of human misery. Only four thousand reached their final destination.

Journalist Harrison Salisbury has called the Long March 'a triumph of human survival'; Edgar Snow described it as 'an odyssey unequalled in modern times'. The marchers themselves had no inkling that they were part of an event that would be as significant to twentieth-century China as the French Revolution was to eighteenth-century Europe or the Civil War to nineteenth-century America.

China: The Long March is a unique publishing project. More than three years in the making, it commemorates the fiftieth anniversary of the Long March by combining the talents of the world's greatest photographers with the knowledge of an experienced and sensitive observer of China. At first it seemed a dream. The problems were indeed daunting. The route of the Long March passed through some of China's most rugged and inhospitable country, through land into which few outsiders had ventured.

Anthony Lawrence, who contributed the text, is particularly well versed in Asian affairs. From 1956 to 1974 he was Far East correspondent for the BBC. English-speaking listeners in many parts of the world received from his broadcasts their first news of the vital changes occurring in that turbulent region.

Central to this book are the magnificent photographs, taken by a group of the world's top photographers, which depict the route of the Long March. The quest for the photographs required months of detailed planning and a preparatory survey. For the actual shoot five Land Rovers, specially shipped into Hong Kong, were used to convey the team to often barely accessible locations. Two hot-air balloons allowed the photographers to capture some spectacular vistas and to present the landscape from a hitherto unknown perspective.

A commemorative reliving of an epoch-making trek, *China: The Long March* takes its readers to the very places where history was made. This book not only tells one of the most remarkable stories of the twentieth century but also provides an extraordinary portrait of China today, fifty years after the traumatic event that shaped its history.

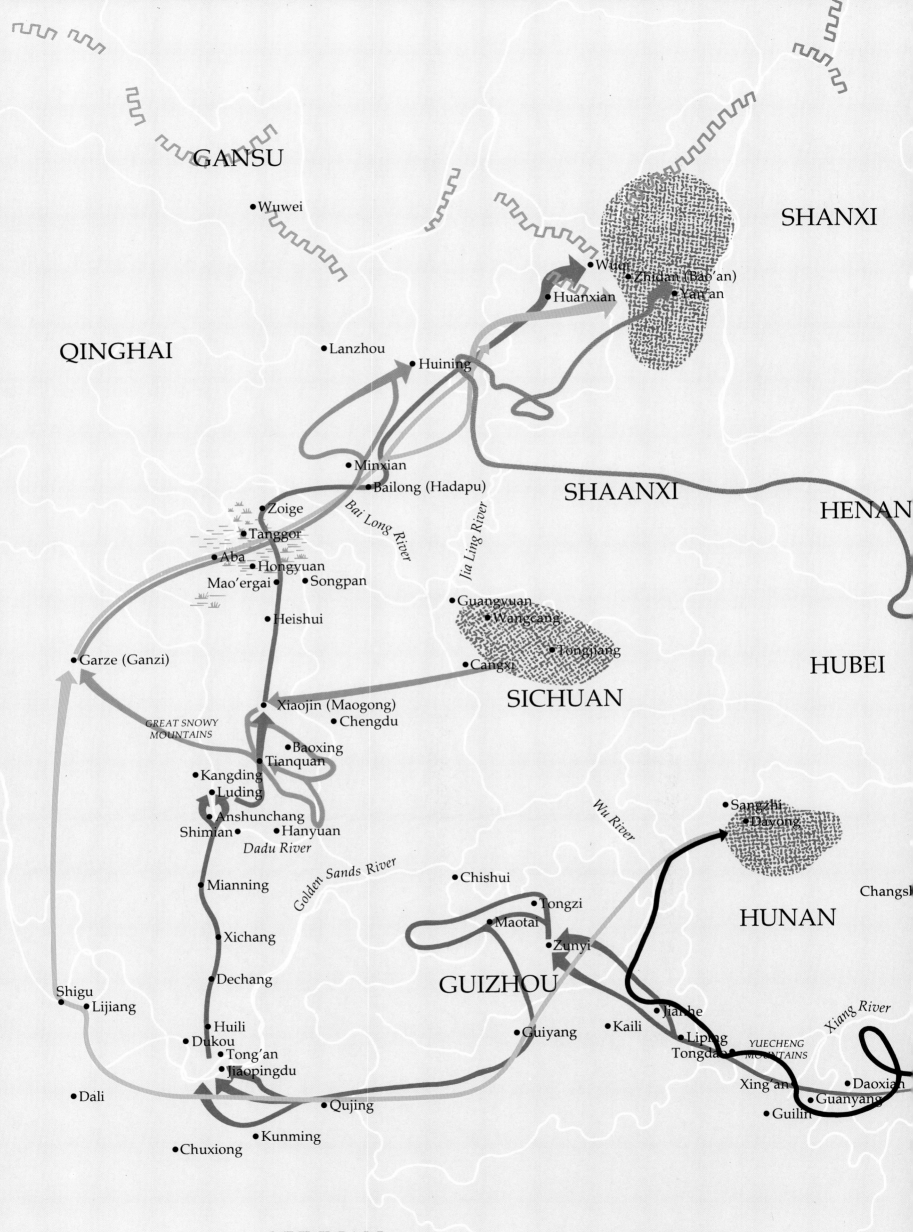

GANSU

Wuwei

SHANXI

QINGHAI

Lanzhou

Huining

Wuqi

Zhidan (Bao'an)

Huanxian

Yan'an

Minxian

Bailong (Hadapu)

SHAANXI

HENAN

Zoige

Bai Long River

Jia Ling River

Tanggor

Aba

Hongyuan

Mao'ergai

Songpan

Guangyuan

Wangcang

Heishui

Tongjiang

HUBEI

Garze (Ganzi)

Cangxi

SICHUAN

Xiaojin (Maogong)

GREAT SNOWY
MOUNTAINS

Chengdu

Baoxing

Tianquan

Kangding

Luding

Sangzhi

Anshunchang

Dayong

Shimian

Hanyuan

Wu River

Dadu River

Mianning

Golden Sands River

Chishui

HUNAN

Tongzi

Changsha

Xichang

Maotai

Zunyi

Dechang

GUIZHOU

Xiang River

Shigu

Lijiang

Huili

Guiyang

Kaili

Jianhe

YUECHENG
MOUNTAINS

Dukou

Tong'an

Liping

Jiaopingdu

Tongdao

Dali

Qujing

Xing'an

Daoxian

Guanyang

Kunming

Guilin

Chuxiong

YUNNAN

GUIZHOU

GUANGXI

SHANDONG

Yellow River

• Nanjing

Shanghai •

Yangtze River

• Wuchang

JIANGXI

• Ninggang
• Maoping
JINGGANG MOUNTAINS
• Gurdong
• Xingguo
• Yadu
Chenzhou
• Rucheng
• Xinfeng
• Ruijin
• Changting

GUANGDONG

FUJIAN

EAST
CHINA
SEA

Guangzhou (Canton)

THE LONG MARCH

August 1934 — October 1936

This map shows in simplified form the routes followed by the main Communist armies during the Long March.

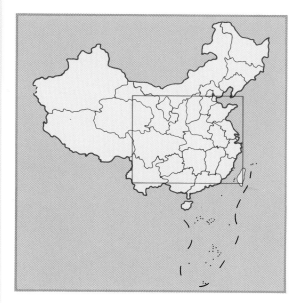

KEY
➡ First Front Army
➡ Second Front Army
➡ Fourth Front Army
➡ 6th Army Corps
➡ 25th Army Corps
🦠 Communist bases
The Grasslands

THE STORY THEN

An Historical Account

PROLOGUE

T HE LONG MARCH of the Chinese Red Army is one of the most amazing chapters in world history. It was a headlong retreat of nearly six thousand miles across snow-covered mountains, marshlands and turbulent rivers in the wildest regions of China. Eighty thousand soldiers of the main force began the march in 1934, pursued by the armies of the Nationalist government, the Guomindang. The enemy was bigger, better equipped and supported by a large air force. Only a few thousand ragged survivors reached journey's end in a remote corner of Shaanxi province. Yet they and their leaders — Mao Zedong, Zhou Enlai and the rest — went on to recruit new strength and in 1949 marched into Beijing to set up the new People's Republic of China.

China was a cruel home for most of its toiling four hundred million people. Despite its size — the third largest country in the world after the Soviet Union and Canada — much of it was mountain and desert. In time of drought or flood, millions perished.

An outdated Manchu dynasty and an evil Empress Dowager had held China back from the twentieth century. They were overthrown in 1911, and a would-be democratic regime was tried and failed. Then the 1917 Russian Revolution echoed around the

★

Left: *The Red Army forded rivers, slogged through swamps and forests and climbed snow-covered heights, seeking a new base in northwest China. They died from enemy harassment, hunger and mountain sickness.*

Above: *A romantic painting of Mao Zedong, Zhou Enlai and Zhu De at the head of the Red Army, braving the rigours of the Snowy Mountains.*

world, and the Chinese Communist Party was founded in 1921. Its fortunes waxed and waned; by the early 1930s its armed forces were in control of scattered areas containing some five million people. The anti-Communist Guomindang leader Chiang Kai-shek determined to wipe them out. For him this was more important than resisting the invading Japanese.

The Communists, outnumbered and outgunned, began moving westward to escape the Guomindang offensive. That was how the Long March began, although nobody called it the Long March then. The Communists were merely scorned as Red bandits on the run. Yet from the survivors came the leaders of modern China. The Party elite in Beijing today are men who were on the Long March. It has deeply influenced their thinking. For fifty years, their sufferings and the lessons they learned on that long retreat have moulded China's attitudes and policies. Mao Zedong summarised those experiences later:

> For twelve months we were under daily reconnaissance and bombing, encircled and pursued, obstructed and intercepted by a huge force of several hundred thousand men . . . we met untold difficulties and dangers on the way . . . we swept through the length and breadth of eleven provinces. The Long March has proclaimed to the world that the Red Army is an army of heroes.

──────────── ★ ────────────

Mao Zedong, leader of the Chinese people from 1949 to 1976, in conference with his old colleague, Marshal Zhu De, the military genius who became commander-in-chief of the Red Army.

CHAPTER ONE

HOW IT ALL BEGAN

MILITARY MUSEUM, BEIJING

THE LONG MARCH is now an official legend, with its own museums, relics and literature. The truth may be stranger; but so many sources are lost, so many voices silenced. Very few of those who survived the march are still alive today, fifty years after. The hardships and heroism, desertions and power-struggles, are all blurred by time and politics. It is often impossible — recalling river crossings, battles, forced marches over mountains — to know exactly what did happen at particular stages of the march, but the basic story casts a shadow touching everyone in China.

Certainly when it began the Communists in China were losing their hold on the five or six areas they still controlled by force of arms. They ran those areas — they called them soviets — on Communist lines, killing off landlords, distributing land among the peasants, indoctrinating, recruiting. Poor peasants, tenant farmers who had suffered rent demands taking half the harvest and tax demands presented years in advance, were often ready to support a collective regime. They were joined by the dispossessed of all kinds — deserters from warlord armies, law-breakers, the homeless. Those living in areas the Communists took over had anyway no choice.

---★---

Left: *Mao Zedong, lecturing to troops, outlines new plans to win over the Chinese people. Against all odds the Red Army survived the Long March, decimated but with greatly strengthened leadership.*

Above: *Mao Zedong and Marshal Zhu De joined forces in the Jinggang Mountains north of Ruijin.*

But guns, bombs and big battalions were the prevailing argument and there the Communists were lacking. One important soviet was just north of the Yangtze River where a famous general, Xu Xiangqian, had built up the Communist Fourth Front Army with Zhang Guotao having the decisive voice as political leader. Under heavy attack by better armed Guomindang forces, they retreated westward in 1932. After losing enormous numbers of men to enemy air bombing, they managed to set up another soviet far to the west, in Sichuan province.

Also under growing pressure was a smaller Communist area around the town of Sangzhi, near the borders of Hunan and Hubei provinces. It was commanded by the legendary He Long, a general in his thirties, hero of a hundred fights and the terror of landlords and officials. Another soviet survived intermittently up in Shaanxi province, just west of the Yellow River.

The principal Communist base, however, was the Jiangxi soviet in southern China where Mao Zedong, farmer's son, teacher, poet and dedicated revolutionary, argued and fought for the leadership of the millions of China's peasants. His close colleague was Zhu De, commander-in-chief of the Communist forces. Also active in Jiangxi were many more who would later play leading parts in Communist China: Zhou Enlai, Deng Xiaoping, Chen Yi, Lin Biao, Peng Dehuai, Nie Rongzhen.

In the early thirties they were scarcely known. The man of the hour was Chiang Kai-shek, national leader, soldier, statesman and sworn enemy of all Communists. His advisers were high-ranking German generals, his resources enormous. When Chiang's forces surrounded the Jiangxi soviet, the Communists had to choose between extermination if they stayed, or breaking out and trying to link up with another Communist area. They broke out.

How did Mao and his colleagues find themselves in this desperate situation? Why was the Communist movement losing out, despite the wretched state of millions of Chinese peasants?

Thirteen years had passed since the first meeting of the Chinese Communist Party, convened secretly in Shanghai in 1921. From the outset, the Communists had been unable to agree on policy. Some, like Mao Zedong and Zhou Enlai, argued for armed struggle; others insisted on a quieter approach.

From early on the voice of the Moscow-backed Communist International (Comintern) was decisive in planning and policy. The Chinese Party lacked funds, membership and, above all, experience. It listened to seasoned revolutionaries from the West — men who could equate Marxist-Leninist wisdom with the poverty-stricken feudalism of the

--- ★ ---

The town of Wuqi, in the loess lands of Shaanxi province, where, in October 1935, the main body of the Red Army ended its six thousand-mile odyssey.

MILITARY MUSEUM, BEIJING

Chinese countryside. The Comintern sent confident Moscow-trained advisers, ready with instructions rarely relevant to China's problems. They echoed the voice of Stalin and sought to ensure that no developments in China would conflict with Soviet interests.

Meanwhile, the Chinese people despaired. True, the deplorable Manchu dynasty had ended in 1911; but what had its successor, the Republic of Sun Yat-sen, brought to China? Not stability and progress, but only civil war, with soldiers looting the farms, a thousand warlords running their petty kingdoms, and huge foreign debts.

Sun Yat-sen died of cancer in 1925; the Communists had co-operated with him and they were working inside the Guomindang when Chiang Kai-shek took over the leadership in the following year. He seemed to offer hope to the Chinese people, with his famous march north to the Yangtze River, defeating powerful warlords on the way and taking over Shanghai. Surely the Communists, in working with him, would share his glory and win the support needed for supreme power?

It was not to be. Instead Chiang, turning against the Communists, ordered them to be massacred by the thousands in Shanghai and other cities. Legend has it that Zhou Enlai missed death by seconds. The survivors made for the countryside or hid where they could. Yet, incredibly, they were instructed by Moscow to launch attacks on cities, to start an urban revolution. The Communists did as they were told, fighting their way into towns with the backing of peasants or rebelling army units, only to be driven out again and hunted across the rice fields and mountains.

Days of contempt. Remnants of Communist units found safety in remote rural enclaves where they set up primitive bases, their soviets. The safest retreats were in mountain ranges straddling provincial borders. Warlords on either side rarely co-operated against rebels and bandits.

Mao Zedong and his battered companies — about nine hundred men in all — found refuge on the forbidding massif of the Jinggang Mountains, on the borders of Jiangxi province in southeast China. This was a wild country of mists and forests, haunted by tiger, wild boar and bandits. Mao teamed up with the bandits, glad of the extra fire-power. Then another motley horde of several thousands arrived — guerrillas with spears and knives, women and children, and a hard core of some six hundred men with rifles, all led by Zhu De. For Zhu hardships were nothing; in the village where he grew up children were often drowned at birth because there was simply not enough food to go round. He had escaped from this rural hell when a rich uncle paid for him to be educated. Zhu had travelled and studied in Germany, fought as a government army officer, taken to opium but cured himself, and later turned to Communism as the one remaining hope for China's peasants.

— ★ —

Artillery units of the Red Army moving through the mountains. All artillery was captured from the enemy, as were most of the Red Army's rifles.

Mao and Zhu were powerful partners. Mao was the thinker who could take Marxist ideas and try to adapt them to China's situation; Zhu translated Mao's thinking into victories in the field. He appreciated and upheld rules of discipline worked out by Mao which respected peasants as human beings. These rules were simple and direct: Obey orders. Take nothing from peasants or workers. Hand in everything confiscated from landlords. Replace doors you borrow for use as beds. Replace straw borrowed for bedding. Speak politely. Pay fairly for what you buy or for anything you damage. Don't bathe in the sight of women. Don't search prisoners before turning them in.

Set out in sixteen characters enshrined in all future guerrilla textbooks were Mao's tactics for victory against a much bigger and better equipped enemy: 'If the enemy advances, we retreat; if he halts and encamps, we harass; if he avoids battle, we attack; if he retreats, we pursue.'

Zhu and Mao worked together and the Jiangxi Communists moved down from the mountains and spread their area of control in the lowlands. Villagers believed there was just one leader, Zhu-Mao.

By the beginning of the 1930s, after the years of defeat in urban uprisings, soviet areas were slowly growing in several provinces of China. The underground Party leadership, surviving dangerously in Shanghai, came to realise that perhaps the one hope of achieving a Communist China lay in remote country areas, working among the peasants. It was pointless for Moscow-trained committee members to quote Lenin on the urban proletariat being the spearhead of revolution. The situation in the towns was untenable. Urban workers might strike for a living wage, but they would not be looking for the defeated Communists to organise or support them — not after the Shanghai massacres. If revolution were to come it would be from the countryside, though the towns might join in later.

★

Chinese Communist leaders in the 1930s.
Left to right: Mao Zedong, Zhou Enlai,
Bo Gu, Zhu De. When Mao's leadership was
confirmed, Bo Gu was demoted.

CHAPTER TWO

BREAK OUT
OR DIE

B Y LATE 1930 it was clear that the Communists in China had survived the massacres in Shanghai and other cities, and Chiang Kai-shek realised that more action was needed to eliminate the soviets and wipe out Marxist thought. In November his staff was drawing up plans for a large-scale campaign of encirclement and annihilation.

Chiang Kai-shek had every reason to think the campaign would succeed. The Communists were poorly armed. They relied almost entirely on weapons and ammunition captured from the enemy. They had little artillery, except small mortars and a few machine guns. They had two captured aircraft, but no aviation fuel, no motor vehicles and few radio sets.

'Three bullets for a charge' was the saying in the Red Army. Only two-thirds of the soldiers had rifles and there was not enough ammunition to be wasted on covering fire. When a battle charge was sounded, on captured bugles, they would rush in with broadswords, hacking and slashing and yelling: 'Kill! Kill!'.

But Chiang, too, had his problems. Despite the successful 1927 campaign which had won him Shanghai, he was not yet firmly in control. Many of the provinces of China

---

★

Left: *An early picture of Mao Zedong, taken in 1933, addressing a conference of peasant representatives in the revolutionary base area of Jiangxi province.*

Above: *A race developed to seize the Loushan Pass, in the mountains north of Zunyi, in early 1935. The Communists got there first.*

were run by warlord chieftains and their provincial armies. They were anti-Communist but not necessarily supporters of Chiang Kai-shek. Chiang's aim was to consolidate his position by disbanding these provincial forces. He aimed to replace them with a single modern Chinese national army under his control, with imported arms and equipment, German advisers and well-trained Chinese officers. But the warlords resisted. They were not meekly going to give up their power and demobilise their troops. Chiang must bargain with them, win their support as best he could, while Japanese troops were threatening China from the north and the Red Army was growing.

Chiang's own Guomindang troops were formidable, as were those of some warlord armies. The rest varied in effectiveness from fair to futile. Some warlords were loyal to Chiang and fought a hard anti-Communist campaign. Others were interested only in guarding the territory they controlled. If Communist forces were simply passing through, they would do little to stop them. For many, a pitched battle was something to be avoided. Generals would sometimes vanish quietly on the eve of an engagement, after having fixed a financial deal with the enemy. Troops were often left without pay, but would get a silver dollar before a battle. 'One dollar and I'll fight for you for an hour', the saying went, 'Two dollars and I'll fight for you for two'.

Some warlord armies were well equipped. Their representatives in Shanghai bought arms from Western munitions salesmen. The troops of Guangxi province were among the best turned out — they got their supplies from Britain and wore khaki uniforms. Yunnan troops were equipped by the French. The black-uniformed troops of Guizhou province were poorly armed and among the least reliable. They were drug addicts and carried opium-smoking equipment in their bamboo packs. In Sichuan province, where half a dozen warlords vied for supremacy, some of the military units were comprised of stout-hearted veterans while others were soaked in opium; some had locally made rifles and others were equipped with arms from Britain and, in lesser quantities, from Germany, France and Czechoslovakia.

It was an army of such disparate elements that moved against Mao's soviet in Jiangxi province. The Communists were greatly outnumbered and the separate enemy columns penetrating deep into Red Army territory threatened their very survival. There was only one possible strategy — to go for Chiang's forces where they were extended and vulnerable, build up local superiority there and hit hard. The Communists launched concentrated raids with telling success. Chiang's main thrust slowed as his weaker units simply melted away.

---------------- ★ ----------------

Above right: *Chiang Kai-shek and his formidable wife, Soong Mei-ling. They stood for defiance of Japan in the Second World War; however, destroying the Communists was their earlier priority.*

Below right: *The men Chiang failed to destroy: a rare picture of the Red Army forces who escaped four attempts at encirclement between 1934 and 1935.*

Three more campaigns failed. The Communists outmanoeuvred their enemies. Good generalship and high morale were often more than a match for warlords who, although anti-Communist, were suspicious that Chiang Kai-shek was out to strengthen his own power at their expense. In a series of quick victories the Communists captured large quantities of arms and many prisoners, who often joined their ranks. By 1933, at the end of the fourth encirclement campaign, their forces in Jiangxi were claiming control of a wide area with a population of two and a half million, defended by an army of two hundred thousand men armed with one hundred and fifty thousand rifles. 'It was the greatest humiliation of my life,' lamented Chiang Kai-shek.

Then things changed. Swayed by success, men abandoned the flexible strategies that had served them so well in the past. In the spring of 1933, the Party's Central Committee moved down from Shanghai and more or less took over the Jiangxi soviet. Moscow-trained young men were in command and at their elbow was the highly capable and persuasive Zhou Enlai. In 1933 he took over as political commissar from Mao, who was seriously ill with malaria. The official view now was that the Communists were strong enough to win any pitched battles; they had no reason to retreat when the enemy attacked; they should never yield. Mobile warfare was outdated.

The Guomindang, too, was using new tactics. Chiang Kai-shek realised an all-out effort was needed to wipe out the Communists; half measures were useless. With the help of his German advisers, Generals von Seeckt and von Falkenhausen, he had strengthened and modernised his armies. He would risk no more hasty attempts at deep penetration; instead he would put around the Jiangxi soviet a noose of steel and fire — and draw it tight. An encircling system of concrete blockhouses was developed, supported by artillery and linked with barbed wire. This network closed in steadily; whole villages were annihilated. The Communists found themselves pinned down and cut off from any contact with the outside world.

Mao proposed breaking out of the blockade and trying to set up guerrilla areas further to the north and west, but was overruled. Instead the loud voice of Comintern agent Otto Braun prevailed (both sides took German advice in this war), insisting that the Communist image would be hopelessly tarnished by any sign of faintheartedness. No retreat: instead, an intensive recruiting campaign through the villages, to stiffen the defence. Braun — his Chinese name was Li De — could speak only German and everything he said had to be translated. But he was a big, confident man who thumped the table and shouted with the authority of the world revolutionary movement. He had his way.

By April 1934, these positional defence tactics of the Red Army caused them serious defeat. That month they lost a major battle with four thousand dead and twenty thousand wounded. The Guomindang blockade was biting. Food ran short; despair spread like a blight. Men deserted or killed themselves with their own rifles. But Mao's critics defended their policies and maintained that guerrilla warfare would have been just as useless against field guns and concrete blockhouses.

Within a few months, the Communist area of control was reduced from seventy to ten counties. Various plans for escaping the enemy encirclement were taking shape. One group was ordered to break through the enemy lines and managed to fight its way north for a while, but was destroyed in heavy fighting. Another force succeeded in joining up with General He Long and his men in western Hunan province.

By the beginning of autumn 1934 the time had come for the main Red Army and government to break out. Rations and ammunition were accumulated and heavy equipment put out of action to deny its use to the enemy. A rearguard of about six thousand troops and local partisans was left to carry on guerrilla warfare, with Xiang Ying and Chen Yi (later to be Foreign Minister of China) in overall command. Ten thousand wounded, or twice as many according to some accounts, were left in primitive hospitals in the mountains.

Where were the Communists going? They had no precise plan, though they hoped to link up with He Long some three hundred and fifty miles to the northwest. There was no time for delay. The blockade's noose was tightening and soon winter would be upon them. Security was essential. Until shortly before the break-out nobody below division command level was told anything. Finally, in October 1934, commanders received the order to move.

In the next two months, the Communists lost half their men.

NO RETREAT!
NO RETREAT!

THE LONG MARCH began at nightfall. The troops left in separate contingents, in a blustering October wind which threatened rain.

In front were two army groups under Lin Biao and Peng Dehuai, warning villagers and checking the areas ahead. Then more formations began to move, soon merging into an army of three columns, with porters, camp followers and a baggage train in the middle — a mass of more than eighty thousand people, spreading along some sixty miles of route.

It was more than an army on the move. With them were printing presses, a mint, sewing machines for uniforms, an enormous store of documents, costumes and equipment for the theatre group, chests of silver dollars and bank notes. Many thought they would be on the move for only a week or two before finding a new base.

The marchers were mostly men in their twenties. Many were veterans of guerrilla warfare and well trained in killing. Most were from very poor families and felt they had nothing to lose by joining the Communists. Many had been recruited from villages in the Communist-controlled areas. Apart from the soldiers there were Party officials,

Left: *Broad, swift-flowing rivers were major obstacles on the march. At the Wu River in Guizhou province, the Communists sent a strike-force across by boat while a pontoon bridge was built for the main body of the army. The river was crossed in two days.*

Above: *In later years Mao Zedong would be depicted as heroic leader of the Long March. When it started, however, he was out of favour.*

civilian porters to carry baggage, and thirty-five women, including wives of the leaders.

All the children, including those of Mao Zedong and his wife, He Zizhen, had to be left behind with peasant families. Those born on the march had also to be left with villagers. Despite exhaustive searches after the march, an infant son born to He Zizhen during the march was never found. Zhou Enlai's wife, Deng Yingchao, was ill with tuberculosis during much of the march. Zhu De's wife, Kang Keqing, was as tough and cheerful as her husband and played a great role urging on stragglers and placing the wounded in peasants' care. Thin and hollow-eyed, Mao nearly died from malaria. Party leaders and some of the sick were provided with horses which were always in short supply. There was no wheeled transport.

The rank and file were heavily laden. As well as his rifle — if he had one — a man carried five pounds of rice. From his shoulder-pole hung either two boxes of ammunition or, if he was an engineer, kerosene cans filled with essential machinery parts or tools. His pack contained a blanket and winter uniform and spare pairs of strong cloth shoes or plaited sandals, sometimes tipped and heeled with metal.

As the march continued, clothing and equipment changed. When there were no villages or towns and no supplies, some struggled on barefoot and in rags. In rich areas they flourished and re-equipped themselves. In places where straw hats were made, they secured big hats made of bamboo and oiled paper. Sometimes they got hold of raincoats made of cloth treated with tung oil, or umbrellas, useful in rain but torn to shreds in hail. Daily rations were carried in a large tin cup, filled with layers of rice and vegetables. Many adolescent boys served in the ranks. They ran messages, foraged for food and tended the wounded.

The initial break-out was well concealed, with local partisans taking over from regular units at defence positions on the perimeter. For days, even weeks, the Guomindang government in Nanjing was not sure what had happened. The Communists broke out to the southwest where the troops facing them were from Guangdong province, ostensibly allies of the government but no great friends of Chiang Kai-shek. They were ready to fight because they feared invasion of their homeland and despoiling of fields and granaries. When Zhou Enlai's emissary assured them that the Communists meant only to cross on their way northwest, the Guangdong soldiers proffered only token resistance. Within three weeks, the Communists had penetrated two encircling enemy lines. Ten days later they were through the third, where the Guangzhou-Hankou railway line runs. They often marched at night to avoid Guomindang air attacks. A Red Army officer recalled:

> Night marching is wonderful if there is a moon and a gentle wind blowing. When no enemy troops were near, whole companies would sing and others would answer. We made torches from pine branches or frayed bamboo. When at the foot of a mountain, we could look up and see a long column of lights coiling like a fiery dragon up the mountainside. From the summit, we would look in both directions and see miles of torches . . . a rosy glow hung over the whole line of march.

But marching at night was too slow to shake off the pursuing Guomindang forces. The Communists soon had to move by day as well. 'With the enemy air-raids we were always scattering and lying down, and then getting up and marching till the next raid came,' said a survivor. Losses were heavy.

The first serious obstacle to their progress was the Xiang River, about two hundred and fifty miles west of the break-out. The river was shallow and forward units waded across without much trouble, but then resistance stiffened. Local troops mistakenly saw the marchers as a threat to the city of Guilin, and fought like tigers. Guomindang divisions moved in from the flanks. The Red Army was split in two by the river and the rear units were slowed down by the heavy baggage train. A tough, bloody battle lasted five days. The surviving Communist forces crossed the river and fought their way clear, but the cost was appallingly high.

Battered and reduced, the Red Army divisions moved along the northern borders of Guangxi province, keeping to the mountains to avoid enemy attack. The going was extremely hard. Sometimes the rough tracks petered out altogether; advance troops were slowed by the terrain. 'Those in the rear would take a few steps forward and then have to wait in their columns unable to rest,' a captain recalled. 'Men fell asleep on their feet.'

The crossing of Laoshan (it means 'Old Mountain') was something no soldier forgot. Rough steps had been cut out of the mountain's steep face, but climbing in the dark was a nightmare. 'The order came to stay where we were until daybreak,' said a man who took part. 'I slept rolled in my blanket on a pathway two feet wide on the edge of an abyss.'

Now they struck northwest, only to face more trouble. Chiang Kai-shek had guessed that they might try to link up with He Long's soviet and had barred the way with many well-armed divisions. If he managed to outflank and encircle them their losses might be enormous. Yet there seemed to be no alternative to pushing doggedly north and paying whatever blood-price the link-up would cost. It was Mao and his supporters who argued forcefully against the plan. Surely it was better to push on westwards, even with no precise objective, than to walk into this Guomindang trap?

Mao's view prevailed, and so the whole direction and extent of this great Communist retreat were changed. Although at that time the Red Army had no accurate knowledge of areas where other Communist forces might be in control, they were now committed to a truly Long March, which would take them a thousand miles to the west and then north, far from the homelands of most of the soldiers. Vague plans to set up a less remote soviet area would be abandoned.

Moving west, this 'First Front Army', as they were called, approached the mountains of Guizhou. This was the province cited in many proverbs for its barrenness and poverty. When a Guizhou family wanted fish for dinner, went one story, the father drew a fish on the wall and the children sat round and used their imagination. The whole province boasted not one pound of silver, not one pound of rice nor, as the marchers were soon to confirm, one level yard of ground. Even Zhu De was shocked at the poverty of the peasants' huts, at the sight of girls working naked in the fields.

The Guizhou provincial forces were opium smokers and poorly led, which was just as well for the Communists, who badly needed a respite. They had suffered devastating losses in the first month of the march. Hardly a day had passed without a skirmish, and the Guomindang's bombers had pursued them relentlessly. By any normal army-command assessment, theirs was a very serious situation. Of an army of some eighty thousand members, only about half were still on the march. The rest were dead, wounded, missing or deserters — apart from some propaganda units, so-called 'dragons' teeth', left behind in the villages and towns along the route to spread the Communist message and recruit supporters. It was a fearful roll-call.

How did the Communist Party leaders sustain the Long March, maintaining control over their men and preventing them from disintegrating into a rabble bent only on personal escape? Partly, it was because the marchers had more to lose by running than by accepting the Red Army command. The enemy took no prisoners. Partly, it was due to the relationship between Red Army officers and their men. Many high-ranking Communist officers were formerly members of the Guomindang and had been trained in the famous military academy at Huangpu near Guangzhou. However, management of the Red Army was along Communist lines. An officer must never strike a soldier. No commander dared to use army supplies for private business. Every unit had a so-called revolutionary soldiers' committee, to maintain morale, organise Communist teaching and handle complaints. And in the companies, especially tough and dedicated men — the political officers — made up a hard fighting backbone. It was they who mostly survived the march.

Communist discipline was observed at close hand by a Swiss missionary, Alfred Bosshardt who, with his wife and a colleague, was captured by Red Army units and forced to march with them. This was a lesser force commanded by twenty-five-year-old General Xiao Ke with Ren Bishi as his commissar. It had broken out of the Guomindang encirclement around Jiangxi back in August 1934 and was on its way to join up with General He Long's Second Front Army. Bosshardt's wife was released, but Bosshardt himself had to stay with the Communists for twenty-seven days of ceaseless marching. He noted how everyone in the marching column had his precise place. This meant that even when disaster loomed there was never any panic. It was a special kind of co-ordinated discipline that enabled an army of mostly illiterate peasants to survive against apparently overwhelming odds.

— ★ —

Chiang Kai-shek reviews his staff officers summoned from various fronts to Chongqing, in Sichuan province. They planned a major campaign to trap the Red Army before it could cross the Yangtze River and swing northwards.

The marching order was maintained even in the dark. When concealment was necessary the lights were doused and the army marched in silence, each man with a hand on the shoulder of the comrade in front of him. As the long column wound on over the mountains, scouts ranged far ahead, marking paths for the main body. The vanguard was the fighting force, but when it met serious opposition the whole army retreated and sought another way round. Once the column found itself back in a village it had left a week before. They pushed themselves to the limit to gain the benefit of surprise. Often they arrived at a defended town when the garrison thought them to be still fifty miles away.

The Communists took the most inaccessible mountain tracks to escape attack, Bosshardt recalled, and the going was extremely hard. He remembered his impression of an endless succession of razor-backed peaks, as he limped along half-crippled with exhaustion. Even tough peasant soldiers wept with the pain of their limbs after a long day's march.

Footwear was the soldier's daily concern and obsession. If he couldn't march he would fall behind, and that was likely to mean his death. No-one had leather boots. Some wore plaited sandals, often in need of repair and replacement. The men with whom Bosshardt marched wore cloth tied to their bare feet with string or straw. In wet weather a pair of sandals fell to pieces in a day's marching and whenever they halted, the soldiers began making fresh sandals with cloth taken from the landlords' houses along the line of march. When they were ahead of the game, men marched with a spare pair of sandals slung over their shoulders.

The landlords were their prey. Landlords were defined as anyone employing servants or farm labourers. Their houses were ransacked and their crops commandeered. Landlords in the towns were fined and their heads hacked off if the fines were not paid before the army moved on.

Stealing from common people was forbidden. One story relates how part of a column sheltered from air attack in a grove of pomelos (large citrus fruit). Although the men were half-crazed with hunger and thirst, the fruit remained untouched because nobody was sure whether the owner was a landlord or a peasant. Finally, a village woman arrived and began selling fruit to the troops.

Bosshardt's unit finally linked up with He Long at the end of October 1934. Bosshardt tried to slip away when the guards were not looking. Betrayed by a peasant, he faced a People's Court and a death sentence. But when told to spell out his name to the watching crowd, the strange foreign sounds of the letters set off gales of laughter — and that saved his life. He was finally released after further months of rough treatment and sickness.

He Long's army, the Second Front Army, stayed in northwest Hunan for several months, harassing provincial forces. This eased the dangers for the central Red Army columns as they toiled westwards into Guizhou in the winter of 1934.

Now the marchers changed tactics. Instead of advancing in a straight line, which made them easy targets for aircraft, they began a series of manoeuvres aimed at confusing the enemy. Two and sometimes four columns followed independent routes, separate from the main body of the army, while the vanguard would sometimes split in two in a pincer movement. Much of the heavier baggage and equipment had by now been abandoned.

When, in December 1934, the Communists took the town of Liping in eastern Guizhou province, they halted and regrouped before pressing on across the broad Wu River to capture the quiet town of Zunyi. According to some accounts, they took the town by subterfuge, without firing a shot. They rested for twelve days, spread propaganda in the villages and won several thousand recruits. Party leaders held a conference — an extended Politburo meeting. The decisions they reached were to have a far-reaching effect on the destinies of both the Party and, later, of all China.

MAO TAKES OVER

THE CONFERENCE AT Zunyi in January 1935 brought the great change in leadership everyone had been expecting. Mao Zedong assumed the top position in the Party which he would retain until his death in 1976. He was not called chairman at Zunyi; he simply joined the standing committee of the Politburo with responsibility for military affairs. But from now on no-one doubted his authority. This visionary farmer's son, who led peasants and wrote poetry, won out over the Western Comintern agent and his supporters.

The immediate subject of debate at Zunyi was military strategy and survival — how to stop the disastrous losses the Red Army had suffered during and since the last encirclement campaign down in Jiangxi; what to tell the political officers; what rallying slogans to give the troops; how to strengthen their fighting spirit. An army of eighty thousand fighting men had been eroded down to thirty-five thousand. Those left were a lean, hard core of experienced fighters, but they were not superhuman.

If morale was to be preserved, command must be transferred to other hands. Why should Party Secretary Bo Gu, just because he had been Moscow-trained, be giving

---

★

Left: *This building in Zunyi was used as the office of the Red Army's political department early in 1935. It is now a museum.*

Above: *Chinese artist Huang Naiyuan depicts Mao arriving in Yan'an in 1936.*

orders to senior officers who had borne the heat and burden of countless fights, when he had never led troops in battle before he came to Jiangxi? Li De, the German adviser, had prevailed over men like Mao, Zhu De and Peng Dehuai, and what was there to show for it but scores of thousands of dead and wounded? Supporters of Li De were reluctant to call a conference at all. They had been discussing the situation only a few weeks before, at Liping. Mao insisted and, on the grounds that crucial military questions would be discussed, he saw to it that senior military leaders were included, even though they were not Politburo members. This helped secure him majority support at the Zunyi conference.

So Mao had his way. Bo Gu and Li De were downgraded and Zhou Enlai frankly admitted to having backed the wrong policies. Mao's was now the decisive voice within the Politburo. Zhou Enlai would from now on be his able and dedicated top staff officer, sharing military command with Zhu De. Supporting Mao were many who would fill positions of power when the People's Republic came into being in October 1949 — among them young Deng Xiaoping, former organiser of students in France and peasant armies in China, and editor of the army's newspaper, *Red Star*. Decades later he would succeed Mao as leader of the Chinese people.

Zunyi marked the point when the Comintern, and thereby Moscow's influence on events in China, was greatly diminished. Moscow's role as leader of world Communism remained unchallenged, and emissaries of China's Communist Party were sent to Moscow to inform authorities there of developments at Zunyi. But communications between China and the Soviet Union were extremely difficult and with the Red Army now retreating deep into China's interior, it was knowledge of men and the countryside rather than politics that best answered the grim needs of survival.

The conference also adopted the slogan 'Go north to fight the Japanese'. Already the Party had been calling for a united front to resist Japanese invasion, which had begun in

---

★

Some of the men who supported Mao Zedong at the Zunyi conference and after.
1. Back row, left to right: *Lou Ruiying; Cheng Zihua; Chen Guang; Deng Xiaoping, then chief secretary of the Chinese Communist Party's central committee, now leader of China.* Front row, left to right: *Wang Shoudao; Yang Shangkun, father of Yang Shaoming, one of the team of photographers who helped make this book; Nie Rongzhen; Xu Haidong, who received the Long Marchers at journey's end.*
2. *Men of the minority group, the Yi tribe, who joined the Red Army.*

3. *Lin Boqu, who once worked with the founder of the Chinese Republic, Sun Yat-sen, and was a close friend of General He Long.*
4. *Red Army commander-in-chief Zhu De.*
5. *Zhou Enlai at the end of the Long March.*
6. *Xu Xiangqian (left), a Red Army general who became one of China's ten marshals after the People's Republic was created, and Ye Jianying (right), later Chinese Defence Minister.*
7. *A group of staff members from the First Congress of Workers', Peasants' and Soldiers' Representatives. First on the left at rear is Madame Kang Keqing, wife of Zhu De.*

1. MILITARY MUSEUM, BEIJING 2. MILITARY MUSEUM, BEIJING 3. MILITARY MUSEUM, BEIJING 4. HELEN SNOW, MAGNUM PHOTOS INC. NEW YORK 5. MUSEUM OF THE CHINESE REVOLUTION, BEIJING 6. MUSEUM OF THE CHINESE REVOLUTION, BEIJING

7. MUSEUM OF THE CHINESE REVOLUTION, BEIJING

1931 with the occupation of Manchuria, followed by more encroachment which would finally lead to the long and disastrous Sino-Japanese War. This Communist appeal for a united front of resistance would prove decisive in furthering the Party's fortunes. It was an appeal to deep patriotic feelings and a growing response came from Chinese of every sort, regardless of politics. They simply felt that the Communists were the strongest anti-Japanese force operating in China.

From Zunyi onwards the aim of the Long March was a link-up with Zhang Guotao somewhere in north Sichuan. This meant crossing the great Yangtze River, a barrier to daunt the most determined of army commanders. The Guomindang forces were not just entrenched on the other side, they were all around Zunyi by now, steadily closing in. Chiang Kai-shek had come down from the north and was in Chongqing directing operations.

The Communists needed to confuse the Guomindang forces and in this kind of strategy the Communists were now becoming masters. It was hard on the rank and file, for weeks were spent marching and counter-marching until the enemy was deceived and shaken off. The Red Army command would make a sudden thrust in one direction and then, after Guomindang troops had been concentrated to stop them, move the main body rapidly elsewhere.

Four times they crossed the Chishui River that flows north into the Yangtze. They occupied small towns near the Sichuan border. They took the town of Maotai, where the famous Chinese spirit of that name is distilled. It resembles aquavit and people say the soldiers thought at first that the colourless fluid in the great storehouse jars was water, and washed their weary feet in it.

After the second crossing of the Chishui the Communists took the strategic Loushan Pass and re-occupied Zunyi, and in the course of the fighting routed two divisions of Guomindang troops. It was their first major victory since the start of the Long March, four months earlier. Hand-to-hand fighting decided the issue. 'We cut them down with broadswords and hand grenades,' said a Red Army political officer. 'The main body fled south. Most of them were wiped out. They had destroyed a pontoon across the Wu River, leaving a thousand of their own troops cut off.' The victory gave a much-needed boost to Red Army morale.

The Yangtze still had to be crossed. It was April 1935 and the Red Army was still in Guizhou evading the Guomindang forces. Chiang Kai-shek was in Guiyang, the provincial capital, checking that defences along the Yangtze River were strong and prepared.

Then a feint Communist attack on Guiyang caused Chiang hastily to summon troops from the west to defend his headquarters. This opened an escape route to the west and gave the Communists their chance to break out of threatened encirclement. It meant gruelling days of marching, but in this region, along the borders of Guizhou and Sichuan provinces, the Communists were getting help from peasants in the villages and workers in the towns. New recruits were joining the march, including women guerrillas who carried ammunition, cared for the sick and repaired clothing.

★

The ferry town of Jiaopingdu, on the Golden Sands River, was the site of the Red Army crossing in May 1935.

Early in 1935 came a shattering setback, though the Communists only learned of it later. The Fourth Front Army, with which the main force planned to link up, had retreated into the high plateaux and mountain valleys of Xikang in the remote northwest of Sichuan province. A further message reported that it was establishing a base area around the town of Songpan. This meant that it was much too far away to be of any help to the main force, the First Front Army, in crossing the Yangtze River.

However, failure to cross the Yangtze would mean tighter encirclement and catastrophe. After further manoeuvres to mislead the enemy, the Communists moved west again. One battalion drew off the Guomindang divisions by pretending to threaten Kunming, capital city of Yunnan province. Meanwhile, the mass of the Red Army made for the upper reaches of the Yangtze, where the river bears the name Golden Sands and thunders down through deep ravines. Here, there were no bridges, and ferries were few and primitive. Chiang Kai-shek was confident that his enemies could not cross.

But by now the Red Army troops were masters of the unexpected. One battalion covered eighty-five miles in a day and a night of forced marching to reach the ferry town of Jiaopingdu, far upriver. They entered the place at midnight without exciting attention and disarmed the garrison. All the ferryboats had been withdrawn to the far bank, but the Communists took a village official down to the river and made him call out to the guards on the opposite side that a government detachment had arrived and needed transport. A boat was duly sent across. It returned manned by Red Army soldiers, who surprised the defenders playing mahjong and seized their stacked arms.

The main forces of the Red Army were swinging north in the wake of the vanguard and by noon of the following day (7 May 1935) they, too, were in the ferry staging area at Jiaopingdu, where they found six large boats. They crossed in nine days, according to the accepted account, without the loss of a single man. When the army had crossed, the boats were destroyed and the troops pushed on northwards.

It was four days before pursuing Guomindang forces reached the Golden Sands River, to be taunted with shouts from the rearguard on the far bank: 'Come over. Try a swim, the water's fine!' according to some accounts. Others say the pursuers met no-one and found nothing save the detritus of thirty thousand marchers: torn fragments of paper, vegetable husks, broken sandals.

The Red Army had shaken off its pursuers, but Chiang Kai-shek still hoped to seal his enemy's escape route at one more strategically important river. This was the Dadu, famous in Chinese legend and history. On its banks heroes of the ancient romance, *The Three Kingdoms*, had met their deaths seventeen hundred years before; only a hundred years before, the last survivors of the once-victorious army of the Taiping Rebellion, led by Prince Shi Dakai, had been destroyed by troops of the ruling Manchu emperor. General Shi had surrendered, only to be tortured and killed.

Chiang Kai-shek wired his warlord allies in Sichuan and his own generals, urging them to repeat the history of victory over the Taipings by wiping out the Communists at the Dadu River crossings. But the Communists also knew Chinese history, and remembered well why the rebel leader had been defeated. Shi Dakai had paused for three days when he reached the river, to celebrate the birth of a son. Those three days' delay had given his enemy the chance to concentrate forces and cut off his line of retreat. As soon as he realised his mistake, Shi had tried to break through the trap but he was caught in the river's narrow gorges.

The Communists did not intend to repeat Shi Dakai's error. No delays for rest or regrouping; they must press on. Some of the younger commanders began to murmur. Forced marching often meant large numbers of men dropping out, with the certainty of being shot when the enemy caught up with them. There was a limit to the endurance of even the toughest.

The dissenters are said to have been overruled at a quick Politburo meeting outside the town of Huili. The race for the Dadu was on, even though the river still lay hundreds of miles to the north — beyond mountains and forests inhabited by minority groups with a deep dislike of strangers, especially ethnic Chinese. These people were the Yis, a tough and warlike tribe active in this western part of Sichuan province for hundreds of years. Chinese officials and armed forces seeking to penetrate the region had been driven out or killed.

However the Communists, unlike their Guomindang opponents, had declared a policy of friendship towards all China's minority groups. There were — and still are today — more than fifty-five of these groups, making up less than eight per cent of the total population but occupying more than half China's territory, mostly remote areas.

The Red Army had already made contact with some of them — the Miao tribes in Guizhou and Yunnan provinces. Where they were able to convince these people that they were merely passing through, with no aim of stealing land or goods, relations were cordial. Gifts were exchanged and the Red Army even won recruits.

The same approach was tried with the Yis in Sichuan. The Red Army captured towns on the Yi country's borders and set free a number of Yi chieftains who had been imprisoned by the provincial administration. These freed prisoners went forward with Red Army units and spoke on their behalf to distrustful tribespeople. The task of fixing an alliance with the Yis was entrusted to Liu Bocheng, a Red Army commander who spoke the local language. He urged them to join with the Communists in fighting the Guomindang. The Yi chiefs asked for weapons. To their surprise and delight, the Communists at once agreed. In a solemn ceremony of brotherhood, Liu Bocheng joined the Yi high chieftain in drinking a toast in blood from a freshly killed cockerel.

The Yi tribesmen proved good friends. They guided the Red Army troops through deep forests which hid them from air reconnaissance and over mountain trails unknown to strangers. The marchers pushed on rapidly and by late May 1935 they were looking down from the heights to a turbulent river far below. They knew it to be the Dadu. The village here was Anshunchang. It looked a very unpromising place for an army's river crossing. Even so, the Communists felt that luck was with them — for some unknown reason, a ferryboat had been left moored on their side of the fast-flowing waters.

——— ★ ———

CHAPTER FIVE

THE BRIDGE OF IRON CHAINS

AMERICAN HERITAGE PICTURE LIBRARY, NEW YORK

T HE RED ARMY'S crossing of the Dadu River by the Bridge of Iron Chains is the most celebrated action of the Long March, recalled in books, operas, ballet and a dozen museums.

It was the second stage of the river crossing. First the Communists hoped to use the ferry to Anshunchang, starting with the boat left on their side of the river. When they entered the village, they learned that the commander of the Guomindang forces was there as, in the mistaken conviction that the Red Army was still many days' march from the river, he had taken the opportunity to visit friends and relatives in the village.

The commander was seized at once, and volunteers were soon using his boat to cross and return with additional craft moored on the far side. For the next three days and nights the ferries transported a full division of assault troops across the river.

By this time the main columns of Red Army forces were arriving, dogged by Guomindang bombing planes. With the limited number of boats available, it would take weeks for the Communists to ferry all their forces across. This would keep them pinned down in the steep valleys — just like the earlier rebel, Shi Dakai. If they could not cross

---

★

Left: *The Luding bridge, over the Dadu River in western Sichuan, was built around 1700 in the reign of the famous Manchu emperor, Kang Xi, and is an important link with Tibet. The Communists knew that if they failed to cross this bridge, their resistance was over.*

Above: *The dramatic crossing of the Luding bridge has been recalled hundreds of times in pictures and legends.*

the Dadu and fight their way north to join the Fourth Front Army, they would be forced to retreat south, into the arms of pursuing Guomindang forces. That promised annihilation. They must cross, or die.

More than a hundred miles upriver was the Luding bridge, the famous swinging bridge made with thirteen thick iron chains — two on each side for safety railings and nine underfoot covered by wooden planks for ease of walking. An entire army might cross in reasonable time, but the bridge must be seized quickly before its defenders could destroy it and reinforce their ranks.

The plan was for the vanguard, which had already crossed at Anshunchang, to march along the far bank and take the enemy in the rear. The main Red Army force would move quickly along the nearer shore and take the Luding bridge by frontal assault.

The two columns set out, keeping in touch by signalling across the river whenever they could. Trails sometimes wound through gorges, climbing several thousand feet, then descending to the river, where soldiers waded through deep mud. Many were barefoot. Despite a night of rain and mud there were only short halts for rest and the cry was: 'Push on! Push on!'.

On the second day, the vanguard moving along the north bank signalled that they had met enemy resistance, and fell behind. The main column kept up its pace and it is claimed that they covered eighty miles in a day and a night. They reached the Luding bridge at dawn on 30 May 1935 and held a council of war in an abandoned missionary church. A mortar bomb crashed nearby; the enemy was ready for them.

The troops on the north bank had still not caught up and nobody knew the strength of the bridge's defenders. The Guomindang soldiers had not destroyed the bridge, but had stripped off its plank flooring back to about forty yards from their side of the river. For more than eighty yards from the river's south bank there were only iron chains swaying over the rushing river below.

There was no time to lose. Red Army soldiers began felling trees and pulling planks and doors from houses, taking anything usable as flooring for the bridge. A call went out for volunteers to make the first crossing. Twenty-two men were chosen and their leader was the young Liao Dazhu. They strapped their guns and swords to their backs and fixed grenades to their belts. Liao Dazhu stepped out, straddled one of the chains, and began working his way towards the north bank, followed by his men. Machine guns laid down covering fire while support troops brought up tree trunks and began laying new bridge flooring.

Mortar fire from the far bank could have wiped out the assault party, but it was too erratic. Machine gun fire swept the bridge. For the men hanging onto iron chains, that was challenge enough.

Liao Dazhu was hit and plummeted to his death. Another fell, and another, but the rest pushed on. As they neared the flooring at the northern bridgehead, they saw enemy soldiers dumping cans of kerosene over the planks and setting them on fire. The sheet of flame spread and some hesitated, but an officer managed to clamber on to the flooring before the flames reached his feet and yelled at the others to follow. They came up and crouched on the planks. Onlookers saw them unbuckling their swords and disappearing into the smoke, hurling hand grenades.

A great cheering broke out as tree trunks thudded into position and a mass of men began moving across the bridge, pressing forward and trampling the flames. 'It was no easy passage,' a soldier recalled. 'There were still big gaps to get over between the rough logs.'

As the Guomindang troops fell back they heard firing in the distance. The vanguard had arrived. By late afternoon Guomindang bombers were attacking the town and trying to hit the bridge, but the battle was over. The way ahead was clear. According to the official version, seventeen men were lost in the winning of the Luding bridge.

Why was the bridge not destroyed before the Red Army arrived? Apparently the defenders thought they would never have to face a frontal assault, and they knew that any demolition attempt would have aroused furious protests among local people. The bridge was a famous, irreplaceable landmark and a main link with Tibet. Before any decision could be reached, the Communists were already on the attack and their volunteers moving forward along the swinging chains.

At a memorial meeting that night to honour lost heroes, Red Army commander Zhu De declared: 'Our difficulties are great and our enemies many, but there is no mountain and no river we cannot cross, no fort we cannot conquer.'

———— ★ ————

DEATH IN
THE MOUNTAINS

BEYOND THE DADU River the Red Army's fiercest enemy was Nature — mountains and swampland, ice and storm. They still faced harassment from Guomindang and warlord troops, savage Tibetan tribes settled in the uplands of west Sichuan, and occasional bombing, but the worst of the fighting was over. So far as newspaper readers in the cities of eastern China were aware, this ragged army had vanished into the wilderness without trace.

The immediate objective was still to link up with the Fourth Front Army in northwest Sichuan. They were not much more than a hundred miles away but it would take seven weeks to make contact because of the natural barriers that separated them. The Communists spent ten days preparing to cross the ranges and peaks of the Great Snowy Mountains, during which time they enjoyed a stroke of luck. A regiment of Tibetan warriors came down from the western uplands to reinforce the Sichuan warlord troops. They wore sheepskin coats and their officers, in fur-lined uniforms, had brought their concubines — women wrapped in furs, hung with jade and, like their masters, riding fine horses. The Communists captured the Tibetans and relieved them of everything, including their horses and the boxes of silver the officers were carrying.

Orders were issued for every soldier to try and carry enough food to last ten days. To conserve energy, troops were to move no more than six or seven hours a day. They had to be prepared to build shelters and use white camouflage in some areas. All frontal attacks on the enemy were to be avoided, any night attacks carefully planned.

★

Left and above: *The Red Army was ill prepared for the rarefied atmosphere, high winds and freezing temperatures of the Great Snowy Mountains, where men died in their thousands.*

MUSEUM OF THE CHINESE REVOLUTION BEIJING

★

Lazikou Mountain Pass, the final mountainous
barrier which the Communists had to face. They
outflanked the Guomindang, capturing the pass
in an impressive early morning frontal attack.

Most thought the Jiajin range the worst. Party founder-member, Dong Biwu, recalled:

We started out at dawn. There was no path at all, but peasants said that tribes came over the mountain on raids, and we could cross it if they could. So we started straight up the mountain, heading for a pass near the summit. Heavy fogs swirled about us, there was a high wind, and halfway up it began to rain. As we climbed higher, we were caught in a terrible hailstorm and the air became so thin we could hardly breathe. Speech was impossible . . . our breath froze and hands and lips turned blue. Men and animals staggered and fell into chasms and disappeared. . . . Those who sat down to rest or relieve themselves froze to death on the spot.

By nightfall, they had crossed the pass at an altitude of sixteen thousand feet and bivouacked in a valley where there was no sign of life:

To avoid enemy bombers we moved at midnight and began climbing the next peak. It rained, then snowed, and the fierce wind whipped our bodies and more men died of exhaustion. The last peak in the range, which we estimated to be eighty *li* [twenty-seven miles] from base to summit, was terrible. Hundreds of our men died there. They would sit down to rest and never get up. All along the route we kept reaching down to pull men to their feet only to find they were already dead.

Most of the casualties were among the southerners, who succumbed to the cold in their thin uniforms. A major cause of sickness was the need to change the diet from rice to *chingko*, a highland barley, as there was no rice in those regions. Eating uncooked chingko caused widespread dysentery and other stomach disorders. Zhou Enlai, seriously ill with fever, had to be carried on a stretcher. Dong Biwu remembers:

I lost track of time but I think it was middle or late June 1935 when we finally reached a broad valley dotted with the huts and tents of many tribal villages and were able . . . to buy food. By that time we had so many sick and exhausted men that our main forces decided to rest for a week while Peng Dehuai led one regiment ahead, to try establishing contact with our Fourth Front Army.

The vanguard was harassed along the route by hostile tribespeople, who rolled boulders from high cliffs down on the Red Army troops. The sound of horns echoed among the hills, calling the local warriors to battle.

Like a hand from heaven for men at the limit of endurance, the vanguard sighted Fourth Front Army units after two days' marching. Recalled a vanguard officer:

We had started building a pontoon across a river when we suddenly saw a column of men running down towards us from the hills on the far side. They were shouting to us, but the roar of the river drowned their voices. Then they threw us messages wrapped round stones, with the names of their army commanders so we could know who they were. General Xu Xiangqian was lowered by rope from the hill-top, with another commander, to greet our general, Peng Dehuai. We sang and wept.

CHAPTER SEVEN

REUNION AND BREAK-UP

SCHOOL OF ORIENTAL AND AFRICAN STUDIES,
LONDON UNIVERSITY

TO THE RANK and file, the reunion of the First and Fourth Front Armies seemed like a miracle. Men of the First Front, marked by the horrors of the Great Snowy Mountains, were renewed by the reinforcement of eighty thousand new comrades from the Fourth. Hopes of Communist victory lived again, despite the steadily falling rain at the welcoming ceremonies and the deep-trodden mud of village roads.

But jubilation was short-lived, replaced by suspicion and open disagreement between leaders, which soon passed down to battalions and companies. It was a contest of personalities. Mao Zedong, leader of the Long March, and Zhang Guotao, in supreme control of the Fourth Front Army, had opposed each other before. Zhang felt his views should carry more weight than Mao's. The men he had led out of the Sichuan soviet were well fed and well armed. They appeared altogether superior, both in numbers and equipment, to Mao's tattered battalions. They even boasted an independent regiment of women, two thousand strong.

Why, Zhang asked, should he pay obeisance to a man who had been part of the

---
★

Left: *Ganzi (today Garze), the small town in the wild southwest of the Great Grasslands where Zhang Guotao set up his headquarters after splitting with Mao Zedong. Here arrived another Communist force, the Second Front Army, led by the famous general, He Long. Later they all marched northeast to reunite with Mao's forces.*

Above: *On the Long March morale was boosted by directives from Mao Zedong and other leaders.*

MILITARY MUSEUM, BEIJING

service staff, a humble library assistant in Beijing University, where Zhang himself had been a fully fledged student? But Mao and his colleagues believed that Zhang's command lacked foresight and Party spirit, that his generals did not understand the appeal for national unity against the Japanese.

At the first meeting of leaders, Mao proposed that the whole Red Army should continue northwards, wipe out enemy units and establish a base stretching across three provinces — Sichuan, Gansu and Shaanxi. At first Zhang agreed, but then he argued that it was better to set up a Communist base in the far west of China, in the wilder minority regions but nearer the Soviet Union. A stalemate followed, hardened by mutual distrust.

It was old army commander Zhu De, greatly disturbed by the antagonism between the two leaders, who produced what appeared to be an acceptable compromise. Let them deal first with the military problem; other questions could wait. Move north to secure the nearest areas of Gansu province before the Guomindang could get there; and then establish a unified headquarters with himself as commander-in-chief and Zhang Guotao as commissar.

This was agreed. The entire Red Army would continue north, but now divided into two columns with Mao leading on the right and Zhang on the left. Some First Front Army units formerly with Mao would march under Zhang's command and some Fourth Front Army units would now be under Mao. Leading the left column, under Zhang Guotao, was the Red Army Headquarters including Zhu De, commander-in-chief, and Liu Bocheng, general chief of staff. More meetings and arguments followed, but the enlarged army continued to move north.

They had heard something of a new barrier they would have to cross — the Great Grasslands; and what they had learned was far from reassuring. It was an area of steppes and broad river valleys some ten thousand feet above sea level. In the rainy season much of it turned to soft, icy swamp. It was a hundred miles across and the only people there were a few nomadic Tibetan herdsmen.

Zhang and his units were to move along the western side of the grasslands and Mao along the eastern side, where there was less distance to be covered. The approach to the grasslands led through wild, deeply forested country inhabited by tribesmen from eastern Tibet. These tribes hated the country's ethnic majority, the Han Chinese. As the Red Army approached, they retreated to the uplands, taking with them all the food and cattle but leaving behind war parties to raid the Chinese columns. Every sheep obtained for food was said to have cost a Red Army man's life.

From the Tibetans' fields the marchers harvested highland barley and turnips which grew to an enormous size in the rarefied air. They did not pay for what they took — the Tibetans were too busy trying to kill them to bargain. Their woman chieftain threatened to boil alive anyone who gave help to the marchers. The Communist policy of friendship towards minority groups would not work here.

The grasslands were worse than they had expected. They suffered bitterly cold

August rains. All around there seemed to be nothing but miles of treacherous swamp, hidden by clumps of rough grass. There was no dry ground. At night the men rested in short stretches, sitting or standing back-to-back for warmth. Worst of all was the lack of food and water. When the Red Army marched it kept to the uplands to avoid enemy attack, but it also needed villages and people — places to buy provisions, spread the Communist word and win new recruits. They normally paid villagers to care for the wounded they left behind. In the Great Grasslands, there was nothing but barren encampments abandoned by nomadic herdsmen.

The exhausted troops, many of them from the semi-tropical south, lacked survival skills in these northern marshes. Much later, northbound units fished in the streams and trapped migrating birds for food, but Mao's army thought only of pressing on to be quit of these mists and icy rains. The soldiers ate wild berries and plants, some of which were safe, others poisonous. There was no wood for fires, so vegetables were eaten raw. They discovered a green root that was crisp and sweet to the taste, but many died after trying it. There was no medicine for the growing number of sick.

'When we came out of those marshes,' a survivor recalled, 'we began eating rats. We cleaned every village of rats.' Forty thousand men of Mao's column marched into the grasslands. The crossing took a week. Ten thousand men never came out. Zhou Enlai was seriously ill; Mao suffered several more bouts of malaria.

Mao's ragged, desperate army broke through enemy lines on the Gansu border in early September 1935 and poured down on to the plains. At last they were among ethnic Chinese again — people of their own Han race. 'They thought we were crazy,' a soldier said afterwards. 'We touched their houses and the earth, we embraced them, we danced and sang and cried to be among our own kind.'

Meanwhile, Zhang Guotao and the left column had started through the grasslands, but radioed that they were held up by flood waters and that Mao should return for discussions. Clearly Zhang was trying to force the leadership to approve his plan of going south. He was secretly giving orders to his units in Mao's column, telling them to bring pressure to bear. Mao left early one morning for the north, leaving behind the Fourth Front Army elements in his column, who rejoined Zhang Guotao.

Soon afterwards Zhang did fall back and set up a base in Ganzi, in the far west of Sichuan. He established his own Party Central Committee, although officers on his staff were most uneasy about their position.

This was the most serious internal struggle and division of strength the Communists experienced in the entire course of the Long March.

supply problems, for this was a poor and mountainous region. They were threatened by Sichuan warlord troops and Guomindang forces led by Xue Yue, a formidable general who had pursued the Communists ever since their break-out from Jiangxi more than a year earlier.

As winter drew on, the Fourth Front Army made a thrust to establish a soviet further east, in the rich Sichuan plain leading to the provincial capital, Chengdu. They advanced to the village of Baizhangguan, a couple of days' march from the capital, but now they ran into desperate resistance and, after a week's fighting, with great losses on both sides, the Communists were forced to retreat into the mountains. Li Xiannian, then a political commissar and general, later president of the People's Republic, managed to negotiate an agreement with local Tibetans to ensure a limited food supply, but it was impossible to sustain a force of forty thousand in such barren territory. For the soldiers of the Fourth Front Army, that winter brought cold and hunger.

In June 1936 they were joined by another force, the Second Front Army under He Long. He was one of the great Communist generals, dashing leader of guerrilla bands, lover of horses, with a reputation for enormous strength and resistance to fatigue. While still in his early thirties, he had already formed and led a peasant army. It was his area of operations that the main Red Army and its leaders had hoped to join after breaking out of the Jiangxi encirclement. That plan had been frustrated. Now, at about the time that Mao and the First Front Army were moving into Shaanxi in late 1935, concluding their six thousand-mile ordeal, He Long and his Second Front Army started westwards on their own long march. They included the force which had broken out of the Jiangxi soviet, led by Xiao Ke, with the very capable Ren Bishi as commissar.

Like the main Red Army, the Second Front Army spent some time in Guizhou province, faced with the problem of crossing the Yangtze River. They took several towns and sought to win over the people. By now, the Japanese were pressing further into northeast China and anti-Japanese feelings were fierce. He Long and his political officers enlisted growing support for a united front against the invaders. They set up a Guizhou People's Anti-Japanese Army and persuaded the patriotic Zhou Suyuan, formerly a high official in the Guizhou government, to be its commander-in-chief. Later he followed the Second Front Army to the north.

In March 1936, He Long and his men pushed down into Yunnan and passed near Kunming, the provincial capital, to cross the Golden Sands River far to the west at Shigu. They had then to cross high, snow-covered mountains. Many thousands died from exhaustion or air attacks, but the army pressed on. In the summer of 1936, they joined up with Zhang Guotao, near the town of Ganzi in western Sichuan.

*   *   *   *   *

Now the world situation was changing. While the Chinese Red armies marched, fought and died in a land of mists and mountains, Hitler had consolidated power in Germany and militarism showed an ugly face in Japan. The nightmare of war on two fronts threatened the Soviet Union, and the Comintern called for anti-Fascist forces everywhere to unite.

This was no time for Chinese Communists to split their forces. In late 1935 a Comintern emissary, Lin Yuying, arrived in Shaanxi. He brought the backing of the Comintern for a Chinese united front against the Japanese invaders and worked hard to reconcile the divided Chinese Communist armies who had been maintaining only minimal exchanges of information and intelligence by radio. Zhang Guotao was told to disband his central committee but permission was given for a southwestern bureau of the Party's central committee to be set up.

So agreement was reached, and it seemed that the split among the Chinese Communists would be healed. Officers and men of the Fourth and Second Front Armies were sick of the mountains and wanted to join their comrades in Shaanxi; and soon Zhu De was leading them north through the grasslands.

At last, in October 1936, at the ancient town of Huining, came the great reunion of all Communist forces, with Mao Zedong and Zhang Guotao on the same platform. The healing of the split and the reunion of armies was hailed in week-long celebrations, with feasting, speeches, banners and slogans.

Now it could be said that the Long March was over, but not the trials of fighting men. Zhang Guotao was determined to carry out his plan to cross the Yellow River and develop a base in the far northwest, nearer the border with the Soviet Union. This had the approval of both the Comintern and the Chinese Party. Units of the Fourth Front Army duly set out, but the operation met with virtually complete disaster. Fierce Muslim horsemen cut down the Red Army forces, wiped out entire companies, raped the women soldiers and sent them to the slave markets. Of Zhang Guotao's once-powerful fighting force, only scattered remnants found their way down to the Shaanxi soviet headquarters.

Had the Fourth Front Army succeeded in the northwest, the outcome of the Long March — and the history of the Chinese Communist Party — might have been very different. There was now no further challenge to Mao's leadership. Zhang Guotao was openly criticised by the Party's Central Committee for having set up a rival body after the split in Sichuan province. In the following year he went over to the Guomindang.

At its Shaanxi headquarters the Red Army licked its wounds, fought off enemy attempts at encirclement and began planning and training for the future. Its losses on

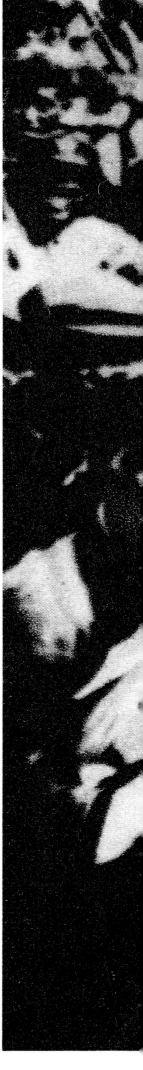

★

Red Army fighters at the end of the Long March, resting in the soviet base area in Shaanxi. The survivors were nearly all cadres — tough political officers chosen for their strength and ideological conviction. These men formed the core of a new Red Army.

the Long March had been appalling. A rough balance sheet of casualties left about one hundred and seventy thousand dead or missing. Soviet bases in various parts of China had been reduced to mere areas of guerrilla activity. Membership of the Communist Party had shrunk to fewer than forty thousand. Yet Communist leaders believed that the general situation was not unpromising. Mao Zedong himself called the Long March 'a manifesto, an agitation-corps, and also a seeding machine. . . . It has sown many seeds in eleven provinces, which will sprout, grow leaves, blossom into flowers, bear fruit and yield a crop.'

Although Shaanxi province was one of the poorest in China, Mao and his colleagues had learned a great deal about organising peasants and collective government. They redistributed land but allowed the landlords to survive. Good harvests were the result.

There was a great need to restore morale among their own troops. Fu Lianzhang, the first medical doctor to volunteer with the Red Army, said in 1936:

A great many of our people now have heart trouble and suffer from nervous conditions because of the strain of the march; and many still suffer from ulceration of the feet and legs. Many died in the Great Snowy Mountains, where the worst problem was mountain sickness because of the rarefied air and the cold.

So many fell sick on the march; and we could easily have saved eighty per cent of them if we had only had medical supplies. As it was, you had to stay healthy, or die. You had to keep up with the column. The sick were always at the rear, never the safest position. Most of the nurses were boys. Teenagers. They were the true heroes of the Long March.

Zhou Enlai said: 'The darkest time in our history was during the Long March — especially when we crossed the Great Grasslands. Our condition was desperate. We not only had nothing to eat, we had nothing to drink. Yet we survived . . .'

New chapters of hardship and achievement lay ahead: guerrilla warfare against the Japanese; great propaganda and recruitment campaigns in the countryside; the uneasy, short-lived partnership with the Guomindang. Then, after the dropping of the atomic bomb and Japan's defeat, followed the feverish years of civil war and the Guomindang's retreat to Taiwan as the tide of Red armies swept across the mainland. Finally, crowning all those years of scheming, planning, exhorting, marching, fighting — at the Gate of Heavenly Peace in Beijing on 1 October 1949, Mao announced the creation of the People's Republic of China. The Long March receded into history, as people set themselves to the thousand tasks of reconstructing China and creating a new society, a new image.

The Long March left scars. All who survived it were rewarded with high command or, in the case of the lower ranks, honourable and safe employment. But the nightmare years of the Cultural Revolution and the Gang of Four (in the late sixties and early seventies) revealed, by the treatment meted out to old colleagues, how much more top-level disagreement and resentment there had been, than had long been suspected.

The influence of Mao's wife, Jiang Qing, and her supporters was expressed in vindictive attacks on many heroes of the Long March. He Long, suffering in old age from diabetes, died after being injected with glucose instead of insulin. Chen Yi was persecuted and his end hastened. The stubborn Peng Dehuai resisted interrogation and torture for months before succumbing. Even Zhu De, the old marshal, was vilified. But now they are dead their glory returns: and the quarrels of the leadership grow blurred with time.

Today, there are probably fewer than six hundred still living who underwent the fearful rigours of the Long March. Many of them, casting their minds back, can recall only a vague, confused jumble of days, weeks, months of marching and fighting and marching again, the gnawing hunger and fatigue.

As for the countless thousands who died along the route, without ever knowing how the battles went or victory was won, their memorial is the line of harsh mountain peaks of China's far west, the chorus of wind and rain over the grasslands, the unrest of great rivers tossing in spray on their own long, long march to the China Sea.

How did they keep going, how did any survive? Ask an old soldier and he will shake his head and say at last, it is all simple enough; you give up thinking and do what the others do. In Beijing an old retired general muses over his time on the march, recites his conviction of the rightness of the Party's policies, then adds: 'But, you see, these were nearly all young men — very strong. They were convinced, although so many of their friends died, all would be well in the end . . .'

Then he quotes Mao Zedong: 'The Long March is a manifesto. It has proclaimed to the world that the Red Army is an army of heroes. . . . Has history ever known a long march equal to ours? No, never.'

———— ★ ————

PART TWO

FIFTY YEARS ON

A Pictorial Survey

THE JIANGXI CIRCLE AND BEYOND

THE STORY OF the Long March begins in China's landlocked and mountainous province of Jiangxi. On its southwestern borders are the Jinggang Mountains where Mao Zedong led his exhausted survivors after fruitless struggles against the Guomindang government. East of the mountains lie the areas the Communists subsequently took over, with the city of Ruijin at the centre.

Jiangxi province, rich in coal and tungsten ore, has undergone considerable change since the days when the Communists defended their soviet against the encirclement campaigns of Chiang Kai-shek. Development has been helped by a sixty thousand-kilowatt hydroelectric station which has provided power for the past thirty years. Some twenty-five million people live in the province and although most of them are farmers, there are also important porcelain and tractor-building industries.

Among the several picturesque old river ports in Jiangxi province is Jiujiang, where there was once a foreign concession area. Significant towns along the route of the march include Maoping and Ningkang, home to large Hakka populations, many of whom joined the Red Army. Memories of the soviet and the beginnings of the Long March are preserved in local museums, wall slogans and human minds. Men and women, now in their seventies and eighties, speak of their membership of the Party in those early days, and recall how they worked with the guerrilla units or shouldered pack and rifle to march with the Red Army.

★

Left: *The Jinggang Mountains, where Mao Zedong and his men found refuge in 1927, are a group of rocky peaks stretching for many miles.*

Overleaf: *Ruijin, capital of the area the Communists took over when they came down from the Jinggang Mountains. By that time their numbers were growing. Today Ruijin is gaining prosperity with manufacturing and sugar cane farming.*

GEORG GERSTER

YANG SHAOMING

★

Above: *The Yudu River in the Jiangxi soviet area, the first river to be crossed by the Headquarters units of the Red Army at the start of the Long March in October 1934. Engineers had laid pontoon bridges across the stream but the water was low at that time and in the broader reaches men could easily wade across. At that early stage none of the leaders had any idea of their final destination. They only knew that, with a powerful enemy closing in, they had no choice but flight.*

Right: *In this small village of Yeping, just north of the Jiangxi soviet capital of Ruijin, Communist leaders held an important meeting in November 1931. This was the first all-China Soviet Congress after Mao Zedong and Zhu De had repulsed three encirclement campaigns by the Guomindang and were providing the Party with its main source of revenue. Zhou Enlai, who had come down from Shanghai for the Congress, was among those who stayed on in Jiangxi.*

YANG SHAOMING

★

Top: *Factory worker in the town of Changting, once part of the Jiangxi soviet.*

Left: *This grandmother lives with her son in a village in the Jinggang Mountains. She remembers Mao Zedong living next door.*

Above: *Chong Jiading, aged seventy-eight, a Red Army veteran, still lives near Changting.*

Right: *A balloon's-eye view of the rich farmland around the town of Ruijin, in Jiangxi province. Balloons fascinated the local people, who flocked along the roads to see them land.*

ENRICO FERORELLI

GEORG GERSTER

★

Left: *The approaches to the town of Yudu, an
important centre in the Jiangxi soviet. Arable
land is scarce; even the upland valleys are
terraced and sown, and the bare hills are being
planted with conifers. From Yudu a large section
of the Red Army began the Long March.*

Above: *In the valleys of Jiangxi province the rice
is green and a good harvest is promised. Here,
where fifty years ago the Red Army recruited
villagers and spread the Communist word,
farmers still till the fields with the kind of tools
their ancestors used.*

Overleaf: *A daunting pattern of mountains
seen from Eight Faces Pass, one of the five routes
of access the Communists garrisoned to protect
their refuge in the Jinggang Mountains. No
terrain, this, to tempt hostile warlords; the
Communists were left in comparative peace.*

Pages 88—89: *The bridge at Longyuenko, near
the Jinggang Mountains, is today quiet and
peaceful. It was once the scene of a fierce conflict
between the Communists, led by Mao's general
Zhu De, and warlord troops — a battle won by
the Red Army.*

YANG SHAOMING

ENRICO FERORELLI

ENRICO FERORELLI

★

Above: The town of Huichang, on the bend of the Xiun River. At the time of the Jiangxi soviet, this was the centre where Deng Xiaoping, now China's leader, presided over the work of the Huichang county committee. When the Red Army pulled out and the Long March began, a force led by Chen Yi was left behind and continued to resist the Guomindang, but Huichang fell in November 1934.

Centre right: A cave in the mountains used by the Red Army, sometimes as a hospital and sometimes as a prison for landlords. The waterfall was valuable not only for drinking and cooking but also for powering the mint. Now only the rare visitor finds the way to this remote neighbourhood.

Below right: China's age-old method of irrigation. The feet of farmers pedal the machine to lift the water from the ditches onto the fields.

Far right: Duck-farming is a major occupation in the plains of South Jiangxi. The Communists took over many farms in this area when lack of food forced them down from the mountains.

Overleaf: The People's Liberation Army of today has changed indeed from the days of rough tunics and soft caps. The hardships of the Long March are the legends of heroes rather than lessons to follow in these days of mechanisation. The military uniform has been updated and the army is looking for better educated recruits.

ENRICO FERORELLI

MICHAEL YAMASHITA

————— ★ —————

Above and right: *Along the route of the Long
March, and in every province of China, in
September 1985 towns and cities celebrated
China's first Teachers' Day. China has almost
ten million teachers. The government believes
that without vigorous education programmes
among the young, China's modernisation policy
can never succeed. One aim of Teachers' Day is
to raise the prestige of the teaching profession.
Long March photographers took these pictures
at Liping and Zunyi, in Guizhou province.*

ENRICO FERORELLI

★

Left: Small children at play during recess at the Zunyi Cultural Primary School. The building once housed the political headquarters of the Red Army. It became a school in 1949.

Above: A bicycle-made-for-four at the village called 'Below the Big Rock', on the slopes of the Jinggang Mountains. In the countryside the bicycle is the vital all-purpose machine for pulling vegetables to market on a barrow, for moving household belongings, or for transporting all the family.

MICHAEL YAMASHITA

ENRICO FERORELLI

ENRICO FERORELLI

ENRICO FERORELLI

Left: Transport and communications are still a major problem in China, and one that is growing more pressing as trade and industry develop. Ferries give way to pontoon bridges; pontoons are replaced by stone bridges to support roads or railways. When the Communists were in southwest Jiangxi province fifty-five years ago this bridge across the River Xiao was hauled to the bank when there was threat of enemy attack.

Far left: The town of Jungyang, where riverboats are built, northeast of the Jinggang Mountains. Along the rivers business was conducted between the soviet and the outside world

Above: On waterways in Jiangxi province, a simple pattern of life persists. Women push out into the shallow stream in tubs to gather caltrop, a kind of water thistle used for fodder.

★

Left: *The room in the small town of Ninggang where Mao came to live while the Communists were establishing themselves in the Jinggang Mountains. It is known as the 'eight-sided tower' because of the cupola in the roof. Mao stayed in this room from 7 April 1927 until January 1929, and wrote some of his early brochures here. Now the room is preserved as a museum.*

Above: *The view from an upstairs room in the small town of Chenzhou, in eastern Hunan province. Along the streets below passed units of the Red Army in late 1934, breaking through the Nationalist enemy lines of encirclement. The speed and effectiveness of the Red Army's break-out was partly the result of a lack of determination by provincial warlord armies. When the Guangdong authorities realised that the Communists were moving westward out of their area, they were happy to let them go.*

★

Above: *Traditionally China is a land of united families. Near Guidong, in the former soviet in Jiangxi province, this three-generation family posed for its portrait and called in brothers and sisters working in the fields to make up the full number. The picture shows grandfather and grandmother (centre back), with their eldest son and his wife and daughter (right). The second son and his wife are to the left.*

Right: *Je Yuangui, eighty-nine years old. Nearly sixty years ago, a sturdy young farmer, he joined the Red Army when it took over Rucheng, the small town where he was born and still lives. He has survived dramatic chapters of China's story — the Long March, the war against the Japanese and three years of fighting the Nationalist armies of Chiang Kai-shek.*

ENRICO FERORELLI

★

Above: *Since the days of the Long March the fields of China have been transformed. Under a personal responsibility system, a farmer contracts with the State to supply agreed amounts of grain and beyond this grows what he considers best for the market. As a result peasants in many places are growing richer, and buying more farm equipment.*

Right: *A young woman makes rattan products, such as baskets, hats and furniture. The traditional craft of rattan-work existed in China centuries before the call of revolution echoed through the villages. Rattan is supple and strong like bamboo, the symbol of the Chinese spirit.*

YANG SHAOMING

YANG SHAOMING

★

Left: When the forces of Chiang Kai-shek launched their fifth and final encirclement campaign against the Jiangxi soviet, the main strength of the attack came from the north and the east. The Communists resisted at the river bank here at Xingguo and then their crack troops pulled back to an assembly area to begin the Long March. Their places were taken by local guerrilla forces who covered their retreat, and for a while the enemy was unaware of the break-out.

Above: Other Red Army forces pulled back across the Mian River at Wuyang, south of Ruijin. It was an operation carried out under steady, ruthless Nationalist pressure. Chiang Kai-shek was tightening a noose of concrete strongholds linked with barbed wire and backed up by artillery. As more outlying villages fell to the attackers, all inhabitants suspected of helping the Communists were executed.

★

Left and above: *A deep, wooded ravine below
fertile rice paddies in western Hunan province.
Part of the Red Army passed through here,
crossing the endless succession of valleys and
mountain heights. The troops paid the villagers
for food, and also for looking after the wounded
and newborn babies left behind on the march.
Landlords were the marchers' victims: those who
employed field labour or domestic staff had their
houses ransacked and crops confiscated.*

Top: *The way over the mountains to the town of
Guidong. During the Long March, this would
have been the roughest of tracks. The
Communists marched with plaited sandals,
sometimes tipped with metal at heel and toe.
Those who were unaccustomed to the punishing
conditions of the mountains soon fell behind.*

★

*An electric storm at Xinfeng, a town on the Tao
River some sixty-five miles southwest of the
Communist area capital, Ruijin.*

THE ROAD TO ZUNYI

I N THE EARLY stages of the Long March, from the soviet in south Jiangxi province to the city of Zunyi, nearly eight hundred miles to the west, the Red Army and its leaders learned bitter lessons. Though enemy attacks could be more easily avoided when they kept to the mountains along provincial boundaries, the going here was extremely hard.

Today much of the terrain is as grim as it was fifty years ago, although rough mountain tracks have sometimes been replaced by roads, radio and telephone links have improved communications, and the number of television sets is growing.

Hunan province, where the Red Army lost nearly half its men at the battle of the Xiang River, has fertile areas in the south which are rich in rice, fish and minerals. Several ethnic minorities live here, including Miaos, Tujias and Tongs. This region has been one of the important crossroads of China since ancient times. The Xiang River, which flows through the capital, Changsha, is the main natural artery of transport.

Guizhou province, which the Red Army marched across, is one of the poorest in China. It lacks flat arable land and is crisscrossed by mountains that hinder communications between town and village. However, the province yields some gold, silver, copper and other minerals, and its tobacco is famous throughout China.

★

Left: *Monument to men of the Red Army in Guizhou province. At this point the First Front Army was about sixty miles from Zunyi. The inscription says that the revolutionary heroes will never perish.*

Overleaf: *Early morning on the Li River, south of the city of Guilin. The local people claim that this area is the most beautiful in all China. But when the Red Army passed through further north at the Xiang River, connected to the Li by an ancient canal, the marchers were too hard pressed to enjoy the view.*

ADAM WOOLFITT

ADAM WOOLFITT

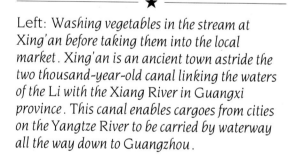

★

Left: *Washing vegetables in the stream at Xing'an before taking them into the local market. Xing'an is an ancient town astride the two thousand-year-old canal linking the waters of the Li with the Xiang River in Guangxi province. This canal enables cargoes from cities on the Yangtze River to be carried by waterway all the way down to Guangzhou.*

Above: *A Yao woman working in a field of sweet potatoes in the Yuecheng Mountains wears a waterproof coat made from palm bark. A traditional way of keeping dry in the Chinese countryside is to wear rough cloaks made of bark or overlapping palm leaves. In some rural areas cloth for raincoats is treated with tung oil.*

Right: *Scarecrow with a red flag in the rice fields near Guanyang, in northeast Guangxi province. The Communists never took it amiss that they were called the Reds and their enemies the Whites. For the Chinese, red suggests virtue and good fortune; white is the colour of mourning and death.*

★

Above: Once the Communists had battled their way across the Xiang River, losing nearly half their men as they did so, they then had to cross the Yuecheng Mountains. Here the foothills were terraced and the rice harvests generally good, but the Communists took away no happy memories of this area. Their route was up rough steps cut into steep cliffs, and the going was hard.

Right: Across the Yuecheng Mountains, on the borders of Guizhou province, lies the Tongdao area, home of a minority group, the Tong, who live in the mountain valleys. Here a Tong woman is seen dyeing the indigo cloth which is a local product. It was in Tongdao, at a conference of Red Army leaders, that Mao Zedong successfully pressed for a change of course. 'Let them march westward,' he said. If they followed their original plan of moving north, they faced almost certain annihilation.

Overleaf: Scene in the Yuecheng Mountains, which the Red Army had to cross after the grim, week-long battle of the Xiang River in northwest Guangxi province. Here the minority peoples are relatively prosperous because of the vast crops of bamboo they harvest from the mountain slopes. The rivers are crossed by high swinging bridges, which the people call 'wind bridges'

★

A pontoon bridge at the town of Daoxian, in Hunan province. When the Red Army arrived here, there were no boats and the town was protected by a high wall. Scouts swam across while others were rowed over, it is said, by local sympathisers. Finally the whole army managed to cross by a hastily built pontoon bridge. When the photographer Adam Woolfitt visited the town fifty years later there was no bridge across the river. Did he need a picture of the bridge? No problem, come back in an hour. 'Certainly,' he recorded in his diary, 'this is the first time I have had a bridge built for me in an hour!'

ADAM WOOLFITT

★

Above: *General store at Xing'an, the town astride the ancient canal connecting two rivers and providing a link between north China and Guangzhou. Xing'an now has a prosperous air and the choice of goods in the local store is far greater than ever before.*

Right: *A Yao woman selling herbs at the market in Tongdao. Tongdao lies in Guizhou province, the home of large numbers of Chinese people from tribal groups. There are about one and a quarter million Yaos in China, all in the south.*

WANG WEN LAN

★

Left and above: *There are about four million Miao people in China and the Red Army met many of them in Guizhou province. Their colourful, much-decorated dress distinguishes them from the more drably clothed Han Chinese; they also have their own customs and language. When, in past centuries, the Chinese pressed down into Guizhou from the north, the Miaos were driven into the hills where they developed a strong hatred of the invaders. Red Army policy was to cultivate the friendship of all minority groups, and a number of Miaos were recruited when the Communist forces passed through Guizhou province.*

Overleaf: *Guizhou province is one of the toughest in China for marching, as the troops of the Red Army were to learn as they tramped along rough roads and stony tracks winding over ridges and valleys. When they reached these Miaoling Mountains they were still less than halfway across the province.*

WANG WEN LAN

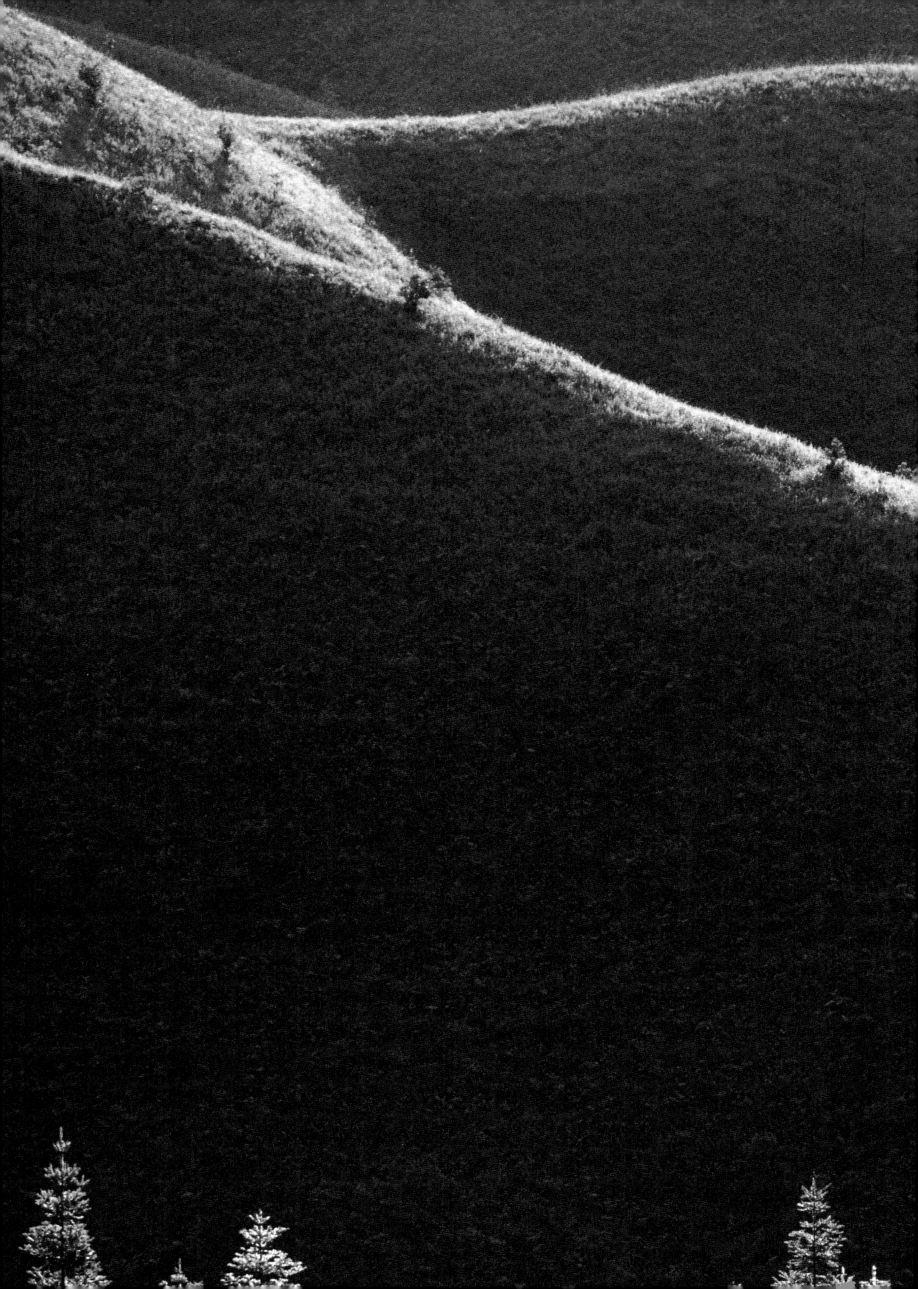

★

Left: *The small town of Wenshi, on the Guan River, serves as a minor transport centre for timber brought down from the hills. The Red Army made its way across this river without meeting major resistance.*

Above: *Wu Shihong, aged eighty-five, is the guardian of the Kougong shrine in the town of Daoxian. Both he and the shrine survived the fighting between Reds and Whites and, more recently, the activities of the Red Guards in the Cultural Revolution.*

WANG WEN LAN

★

Above: *Conditions in Guizhou have much improved. The rice crop at Chong'an, in the hills fifty miles west of Jianhe, in Guizhou province, has been particularly good in recent years.*

Right: *A cattle fair at Jianhe on the road to Zunyi. Lean, spare-ribbed beasts have been driven here for sale by the Miao farmers wearing their distinctive hats. It was the poverty of Guizhou province that first struck the Red Army as it passed through fields and villages seeking provisions and recruits. In 1934 the only flourishing industry seemed to be opium and the vast majority of the population were addicts.*

Overleaf: *Washing vegetables in the river at Huaxi, in Hunan province. The shoulder-pole is still the usual means of transporting goods, including Chinese lettuces, cabbages and red chillies, to market. But the watch on the woman's wrist shows how things have changed since the Red Army passed through this area more than fifty years ago.*

WANG WEN LAN

MICHAEL YAMASHITA

———————————— ★ ————————————

Above: *The easiest way to thresh the rice is to beat the stalks on a platform protected from the wind by a screen.*

Right: *Terraced rice fields near Liping, in eastern Guizhou province. By the time the Red Army passed through here, the harvest was in. When the photographers of the Long March team visited Liping, the paddy was cut and the sheaves stacked in the fields to dry before threshing. In Guizhou every new foot of rice-growing land has to be carved out of the hills. Irrigation is a complex problem; the water is drained down from the top fields so that each plot receives the flooding it needs. In some parts of China the land yields two, and even three, rice crops annually, but in Guizhou it gives only one crop. Conditions will improve with the increased use of fertilisers and pesticides.*

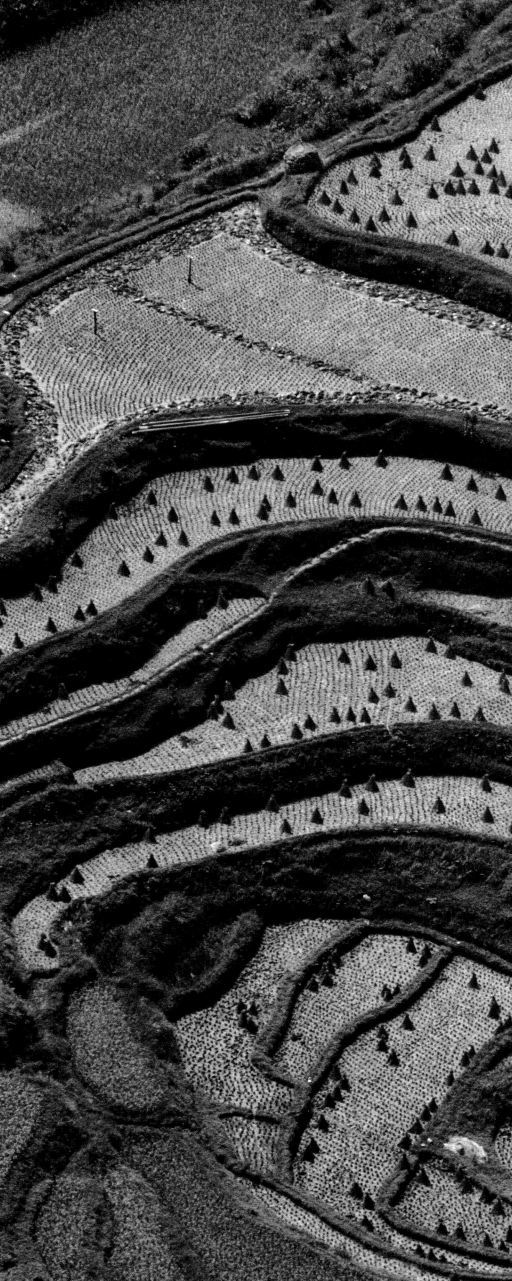

GEORG GERSTER

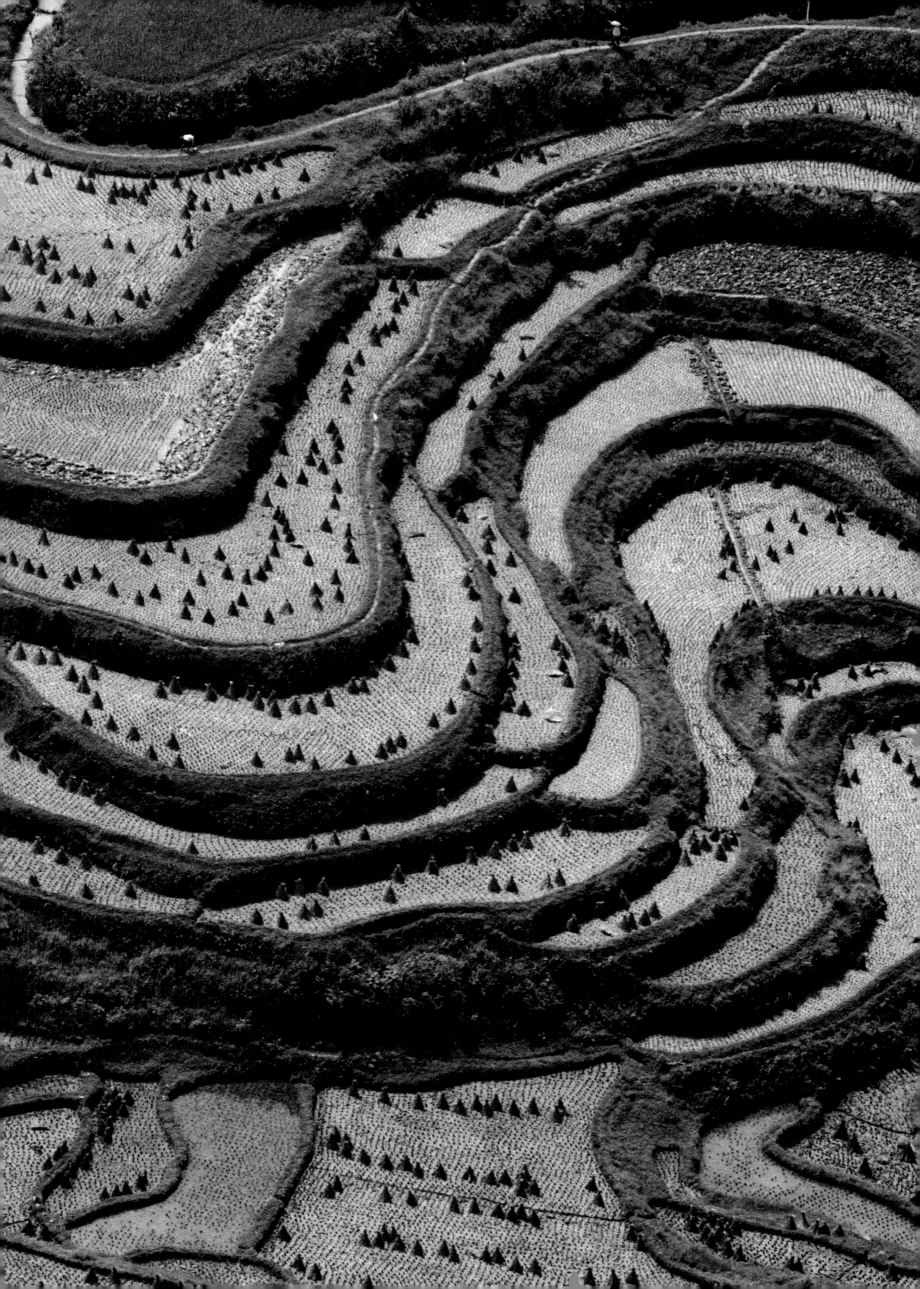

Above: Guiyang today, the capital of Guizhou province, with the mountains beyond. Here Chiang Kai-shek set up his headquarters early in 1935 and ordered the movements of Nationalist armies aiming to squeeze the Communist forces in a trap while they were attempting to cross the Yangtze River and move north. But he was confused by the rapid manoeuvring of the Red Army. At one point Chiang was sure Guiyang itself was threatened. Then, when forces had been hastily summoned to the defence of the city, he heard that the Communists had moved west and eluded Nationalist encirclement.

Right: Aerial view of the Red Army memorial at Zunyi. When the Communist troops left Zunyi they were a very different fighting force from the unwieldy, barely manageable horde who had streamed out of the soviet in Jiangxi province some two months before. By now they were a lean, tough body of some thirty thousand men. They had suffered continual attacks from enemy air and ground forces, and had lost many men through death, wounds and desertion. But they had also won their first considerable victory, at the Wu River, south of Zunyi. Gradually, too, the Long March was becoming less of a headlong retreat and more of a large-scale military project.

MICHAEL YAMASHITA

MICHAEL YAMASHITA

★

Left: *The Wu River electric power plant, near Zunyi, in Guizhou province. All the power in this rocky, mountainous province is provided by hydroelectric plants like this. In the old days Guizhou yielded little food or wealth — apart from opium. The worse the condition of the people, the more they took to smoking opium to relieve their misery. Today industry is burgeoning, for the province is rich in coal and iron and other minerals. The government plans to develop mining and industry on a still greater scale and to attract foreign investment.*

Above: *Meanwhile, large areas of the province look much as they did fifty years ago when the Red Army marched through. But now, in many places, roads have replaced rough tracks, the people are adequately clothed, and the towns have developed into cities.*

Right: *Small boys don't change.*

MICHAEL YAMASHITA

★

Above: *The Yianging River valley as it approaches Zunyi. The grim mountain ridges of Guizhou dominate the scene today as they did when the Red Army slogged its way through. But here and there primitive village dwellings have been replaced by more modern housing. The commune system has virtually been abandoned and peasants are urged to use their initiative to grow profitable crops. Now the man with a hard-working family can double or treble his income.*

Right: *Does the road wind uphill all the way? Yes, it does, except that in the days of the Long March there was no road over these mountains on the way across Guizhou, and the Red Army troops climbed by rough tracks. When they reached a summit, in front stretched another high ridge, and more beyond. Improving the road system has been one of the major tasks facing Communist provincial administrations.*

★

Long March veterans in Zunyi. The man, Kung Xianquan, was wounded early in 1935. The woman, Li Xiaoxia, was second-in-command of a guerrilla group.

★

Wan Shaolian now lives at the town of Tapingdu, on the Guizhou-Sichuan border. He endured the entire Long March.

———————— ★ ————————

Above: *In the mountains north of Zunyi, where the Red Army passed through, a cheerful woman grinds corn just as her ancestors did.*

Right: *In a farm not far from the village of Xintianwan a woman brings in a load of wild plants to be used for fodder or perhaps for herbal medicines. In this part of China women work in the fields as well as in the house.*

Far right: *The Chishui River near Tucheng, one of the places where the Red Army crossed in their prolonged efforts to shake off threatening Guomindang forces northwest of Zunyi and make their way into Sichuan province. Altogether the Communists crossed the Chishui River four times.*

★

Left: *At the Loushan Pass in February 1935,
the Red Army smashed down into Nationalist
forces trying to ascend the pass and destroyed
whole divisions. The Loushan Pass commanded
the approach to Zunyi and was only lightly
defended by the Nationalists. The Communists
and large enemy reinforcements were each about
the same distance away — some eleven miles. It
was a race to the top of the pass, and the
Communists were there first with just a few
minutes to spare. The battle was continued south
of Zunyi. Nearly two thousand troops were cut
off north of the Wu River and surrendered with
their weapons. Now a busy hard-top road runs
over the Loushan Pass; when the Red Army jog-
trotted to the top early in 1935, they found only
dirt and gravel.*

Above: *Mountains near the coal-mining town
of Malin, in northern Guizhou. The terrain of
this province has held back development and
made communication between towns difficult.*

THE ROAD TO ZUNYI   149

★

Left: *An enormous statue of Mao Zedong broods over Guiyang, capital of Guizhou province. Today Guiyang is an industrial city of seven hundred thousand people, many of whom work in the cement and steel plants.*

Top and above: *The house of the wealthy merchant in Zunyi where the Red Army leaders held their extended Politburo meeting in January 1935. This meeting, which was to confirm Mao as Communist leader, lasted several days and was sometimes heated.*

MICHAEL YAMASHITA

MICHAEL YAMASHITA

PAUL LAU

★

Left: *The Zunyi silk factory is the largest in Guizhou province and employs eighteen hundred workers, mainly women.*

Top and above: *When the Communists took over China, silk production was at an all-time low. Today Chinese exports of raw silk make up about eighty per cent of the world's total silk trade, while Chinese silk fabrics account for forty per cent. At present the Chinese silk industry is undergoing a process of thorough modernisation. Silk mills are now allowed to keep their profits and farmers are encouraged to cultivate silkworms as a sideline.*

FROM THE HEARTLANDS

I N THE EARLY thirties there were several other Communist-controlled areas in China besides the Jiangxi soviet run by the Party leaders. One was in east Sichuan and another in northwest Hunan.

These areas still consist mainly of farmland and are peopled by ethnic minorities. When the Communists were operating in southern Sichuan the main crop was opium and addiction to the drug was widespread. Happily, and the opium habit has long since been stamped out. Today, the southern part of the province boasts lumber, salt, sugar chemical industries and factories manufacturing electrical equipment and machine tools.

Sichuan has a rich and ancient history. In the third century, when China was split into three kingdoms, Sichuan (or the Kingdom of Shu, as it was then known) survived gloriously against its enemies, partly because the high mountains around its boundaries acted as natural defences.

Through Sichuan flows the Yangtze, the longest river in China, linking the province to the big industrial cities of Wuhan and Shanghai. Sichuan is the native province of many revolutionary leaders of the modern age, including Chairman Deng Xiaoping.

---- ★ ----

Left: *This grass-cutter on the hills above Tongjiang, in northeast Sichuan, uses a giant lotus leaf as protection against the weather.*

Overleaf: *The Tianzi Mountains, in northwest Hunan, in the soviet run by the Communist General He Long. Originally the leaders of the Long March had hoped to link up with He Long, but heavy enemy forces blocking the way caused them to abandon this plan and prolong their march by thousands of miles.*

—————— ★ ——————

Left: *Early morning mist over the rice fields in Yongshun county, in northwest Hunan province.*

Top: *Many people of the Tujia minority group live in this part of Hunan. Here two of them are seen unloading winter melon.*

Above: *Today more pigs are raised by individual farmers than by communes.*

Overleaf: *The town of Cangxi, on the Jialing River in Sichuan, was part of the Communist Fourth Front Army's base from 1932 to 1935.*

ZHANG HE SONG

ZHANG HE SONG

★

Above: *Elderly relatives of those who gave their lives for the Communist cause now spend their remaining years in a home for the aged in Tawo district, north Hunan.*

Left: *A veteran soldier of the Second Front Army tells of the meeting of He Long and Xiao Ke and their troops in October 1934 at Muhuang, in northeast Guizhou.*

Right: *In October 1934 General He Long joined the Communist Sixth Army under Xiao Ke at Muhuang. On his way there He Long and his troops crossed the mountains by this path, which is typical of many in the area.*

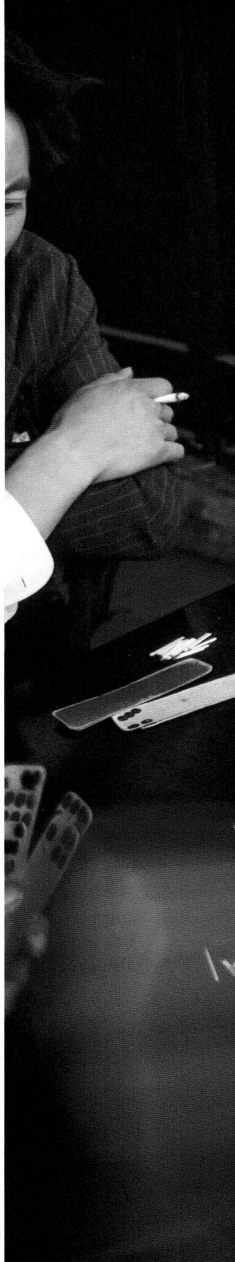

PAUL LAU

★

Above: *An old woman in Wangcang, northeast Sichuan, making shoes. In most rural districts of China the women of the house make shoes by sewing layer upon layer of felt or thick cotton together and joining it to the cut-out uppers.*

Right: *Old men playing cards in a teahouse in Guangyuan, northeast Sichuan, where once the Communist Fourth Front Army had its base.*

Overleaf: *This cement-making plant near Wangcang is typical of the thousands of small enterprises established in recent years to raise the income of farmers and at the same time increase the spread of industry.*

PAUL LAU

Two veterans of the historic battles, photographed in the museum at Wangcang, in the Fourth Front Army's soviet in northeast Sichuan. Lun Hingtsia (above), now seventy-four, was a radio operator. Yang Bin (right), aged sixty-five, served in the ranks as a boy of fifteen.

★

*Left and above: Coins and a bank note
issued by the Fourth Front Army in its soviet in
northeast Sichuan. Some of the coins are of
silver, and are stamped with the hammer and
sickle. The face of Lenin is on the bank note.
When the Fourth Front Army, led by Zhang
Guotao and Xu Xiangqian, arrived in this area
after retreating from a much larger and richer
region near the Yangtze River, the troops were
appalled by the state of the local economy and the
living conditions of the people. For the first six
months there was no question of setting up an
effective government; they were too busy fighting
local warlords. But gradually confidence was
created, both in the Communists and their
currency. It lasted two and a half years, until the
Fourth Front Army was forced to retreat further
to the west. There it was later to be joined by Mao
Zedong and the army of the Long March.*

APPROACH TO LUDING

WHEN THE SOLDIERS of the Red Army marched south from Guizhou province into Yunnan ('South of the Clouds') they left one of the dullest and wettest regions of China for a land of almost unbroken spring sunshine. The provincial capital, Kunming, around which Communist units manoeuvred to mislead their enemies, is still a city of magnolias, azaleas and subtropical fruit; but now it also has factories producing electrical equipment, machine tools and motor vehicles, as well as cement, fertilisers and chemicals.

The lifestyle of the Yunnan people is changing as they are exposed to the outside world. But the people of the area's many minority groups still wear their bright costumes and celebrate traditional festivals. Out of some fifty such groups, spread thinly over China's western expanses, about twenty are concentrated in Yunnan, making up about one third of the province's thirty million inhabitants.

Yunnan is situated on a large plateau with an average height of more than four thousand feet above sea level. It shares borders with Burma, Laos and Vietnam, across which informal trade takes place.

For many years development of industry in Yunnan was held up because of difficulty of access from central China, though there is now a direct rail link with Chengdu, in Sichuan province. Tin is mined in southeastern Yunnan, where there are also resources of coal and iron ore.

★

Cascading waterfall in the Luoji Mountains.

MARY ELLEN MARK

★

Left: *An old woman in Lutu village, in the mountains of Yunnan province, with her two grandchildren. Her feet were bound when she was a young girl. The custom was widely practised among the Chinese until the early years of the twentieth century, when social reformers and revolutionaries campaigned against it. In earlier days foot-binding, like tight-lacing in the West, was considered a female attraction. Without it a girl would be a liability in the marriage market; her family would have difficulty in finding her a husband. One of the thirty-five women who took part in the Long March had bound feet.*

Above: *Today, a girl is spared the old barbarous aids to beauty. Instead she may choose a permanent wave at the village hairdresser, with rubber tubes leading from a bowl of boiling water to provide the heat.*

★

This page and the two previous spreads (pages 176-177 and 178-179) were photographed at two funerals in Yunnan province. The first spread shows grieving relatives wearing the traditional mourning colour of white. The second spread depicts the anguish of a young relative. On this page, as a mark of respect, mourners prostrate themselves under the coffin as pallbearers carry it to the burial ground. Earlier, they crawled to the nearest source to collect water. This was blessed by a Taoist priest and then used by the eldest male relative to wash the body of the deceased. After the funeral procession, the coffin will be placed on the ground and covered with a mound of earth.

★

Top: *A proud father with his children in Lutu village, Yunnan province*.

Above: *A country road in Yunnan province*.

Right: *In Qujing, Yunnan, just over the border from Guizhou, young Jing Chungding nurses her baby in hospital*.

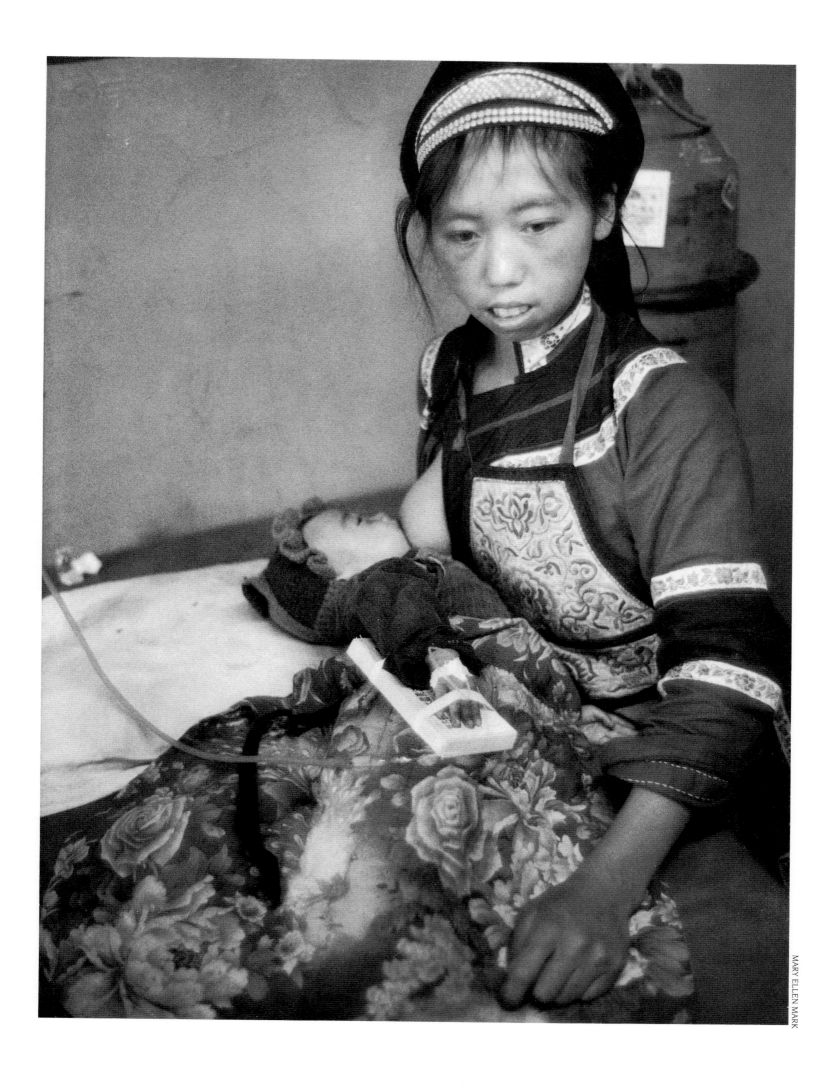

Above: Yang Quam is a painter in the traditional Chinese manner, though he himself is a member of the Bai people. There are one million Bais in China, nearly all of whom are in Yunnan province, in and around the city of Dali. Yang Quam is seen here in his Dali workroom with his two daughters. The taller girl is Yang Daxou, aged twenty-two, a photographer. Her younger sister, aged nineteen, teaches English at a local middle school. They are both wearing Bai national dress.

Right: An old man in Chuxiong city, Yunnan province.

Far right: This young man, encountered in Yunnan's Jianzhou county, is a mute. Strangers are impressed by his gentle character and enigmatic expression.

HANS VERHUFEN

HANS VERHUFEN

GREGORY HEISLER

★

Far left: *Gateway of old Lijiang city, in west Yunnan province. The Second Front Army of He Long passed through here before crossing the Golden Sands River on its own long march north.*

Left: *The cave at Jiaopingdu, on the north side of the Golden Sands River, where Mao Zedong sheltered overnight after crossing the river with the headquarters staff. The inscription reads: 'Long Live Chairman Mao'.*

Below left: *It took nine days for all the units of the Red Army to cross the river; the current runs swiftly here and boats were few. But the hills made it virtually impossible for the pursuing Guomindang to carry out bombing attacks.*

Bottom left: *Mr Feng, Party leader in the Nine Dragons district near Xundian, northeast of Kunming, capital of Yunnan.*

HANS VERHUFEN

HANS VERHUFEN

★

Top: *Behind the shop window bright with scarlet propaganda, an apprentice watchmaker practises his skills.*

Above: *In most minority areas the people show a love of colour and decoration. They paint the walls of houses in intricate patterns and cultivate flowers; even the common bicycle is transformed.*

Right: *In Dukou this young poster artist has been illustrating the friendship between the minority people (represented by the girl in the headdress) and the People's Liberation Army.*

Overleaf: *A field of giant sunflowers near Dali, in Yunnan province.*

Pages 192-193: *By the Qingsheixiang lake, in Yongsheng county, a sudden break in the clouds illuminates the meticulously tended fields.*

HANS VERHUFEN

★

Left: *Road repairers of the Bai nationality at work near Dali, in Yunnan province.*

Top: *The national school at Lijiang, near the Golden Sands River, where the Second Front Army passed through in April 1936. The present school was established in 1982 and its three hundred students are from ten nationalities including Han, Zhuang, Bai, Miao, Naxi, Lisu, Yi and Hui. Each has its own customs, language and dress.*

Above: *Headdress worn by men of the Miao nationality.*

GREGORY HEISLER

GREGORY HEISLER

★

Left: A country road near Shigu, on the Golden Sands River.

Above: A monument at Shigu, erected in 1972 to commemorate the crossing of the river by the Second Front Army in April 1935. About twenty thousand men were transported safely across, without resistance from enemy forces. As survivors of this part of the Long March recall, the going here was generally easy.

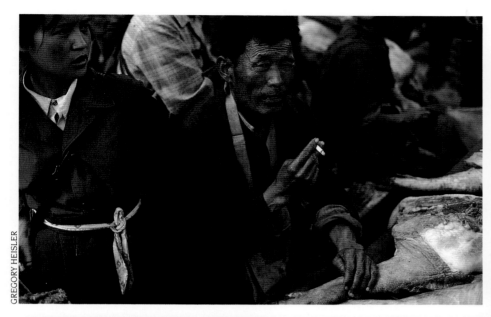

GREGORY HEISLER

GREGORY HEISLER

GREGORY HEISLER

GREGORY HEISLER

★

Life in Yunnan province.

Far left: *Brickmakers in a storage barn near Dali.*

Above: *Gue Jiming testing components in a medicine factory at Lijiang.*

Top left: *Market scene at Dali.*

Centre left: *This silk factory near Chuxiong turns out thirty-two tons of silk annually, ten tons of which is for export. The factory provides jobs for more than a thousand workers.*

Bottom left: *The word on the wall is 'soul'. The Lijiang sign painter is finishing the slogan for Teachers' Day: 'Teachers are the engineers of the human soul'.*

Famous in Yunnan province is the Song and
Dance Troupe of Chuxiong Yi autonomous
prefecture. One of its best known productions is
the dance drama of the Yi people called 'Miyilu',
which is the name of a local flower. The Yi actress
Yiao Qun, aged twenty-one, plays the star role.
The part of the evil despot is played by Han
Chinese actor Qian Ruhua.

Left: A retired Red Army officer, Wang Yinguan, aged seventy-four, in a street of Chuxiong city, Yunnan, where he was born. A Han Chinese by race, he started life as a peasant but joined the Red Army when he was twenty years old. He retired in 1963 and a small building was erected by the local authorities in recognition of his services.

★

Above: *Three veterans of the Long March meet at the bridge of Nanxunqiao, near the Golden Sands River, scene of scattered fighting fifty years ago when the Second Front Army was preparing to cross. From left, Ji Feiquan, Wan Wenhuan and Yu Zhijiang.*

Overleaf: *A steam train near Dukou, on the Golden Sands River, emptying fluid slag from containers. Today Dukou is one of China's iron and steel centres.*

Pages 206-207: *Political meeting in Tong'an, on the north side of the Golden Sands River, Sichuan province. Mao Zedong stayed here overnight after advance units of the Red Army had been safely ferried across the river.*

DI XIANG HUA

DI XIANG HUA

HANS VERHUFEN

★

Far left: *In the Luoji Mountains*.

Above: *Bathers in a pool near Mianning, a town through which the Red Army passed on its march north to the Luding bridge*.

Left: *A young girl in Tong'an market*.

Above: *A woman of the Yi nationality*.

Right: *A street dentist in Qujing*.

Far right: *A Lisu woman in her national dress*.

DI XIANG HUA

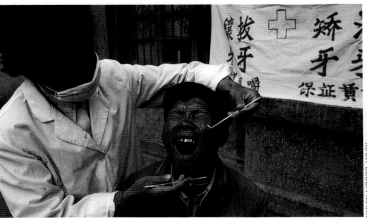

MARY ELLEN MARK

DI XIANG HUA

★

Left: *The Huili Catholic Church. Before the Cultural Revolution (1966-76) there were some two thousand Catholics in Huili, but by the end of the revolution the number had fallen to two hundred. The church building, closed for years, is once again open for services, attended by about sixty people. Because the number of Catholics in Huili has declined, the church has been obliged to sell part of its land to the city government.*

Above: *A Yi village near Dechang, a town which the Red Army marched through in 1935 on its way north to the Dadu River and the Luding bridge.*

THE
SNOWY MOUNTAINS

A S THE LONG March continued through China's far western regions, the First Front Army faced less danger from enemy pursuit and encirclement but suffered more from the rigours of the climate and the hazards of river and mountain. In this area of China the altitude increases as the land slopes upward from east to west until it approaches Tibet, the roof of the world. Tibetans and other ethnic minorities inhabit this region, which in historical times was a frequent source of rebellion against the central imperial government. The capital, Chengdu, controls the main access road from Sichuan into Tibet.

Among the formidable mountains of northwestern Sichuan province nestles the little town of Luding, whose famous Bridge of Iron Chains was for many decades an important link with Tibet. Soon after their dramatic crossing of the bridge, the Communists had to tackle the group of peaks rising to twenty thousand feet known as the Great Snowy Mountains.

This mountainous region, through which the Communists marched in order to link up with their comrades of the Fourth Front Army, presents a sharp contrast with the fertile plains lying further to the east which give Sichuan its fame as one of the richest farming areas of China. Rice, winter wheat, citrus fruits, bamboo and many other crops flourish here.

★

Grand monument to the men of the Red Army
who forced the crossing of the Dadu River
at the Anshunchang Ferry in May 1935.

★

Left: *Dadu River boatmen who ferried Red Army units across the river in May 1935.*

Overleaf: *Luoji village, near the town of Shimian. High hedges separate the rice plots.*

HARALD SUND

★

Right: *The Bridge of Iron Chains over the Dadu
River at Luding, in west Sichuan province.
Under fire, assault troops of the Red Army
crossed by the chains after the enemy had
removed the wooden planks. For two centuries
the bridge was the main link with Tibet. In recent
years a modern bridge has been built near
Luding and now carries most of the traffic. But
the Bridge of Iron Chains remains a famous
landmark, swaying high above the waves and
whirlpools of the fast-running Dadu in a single
span of a hundred yards. It was built in 1705,
during the reign of the Manchu emperor, Kang Xi.*

Above: *In Kangding, across the bridge,
workmen fell trees on the mountain slopes and
float the timber downriver to the sawmills.*

Overleaf: *The Luding bridge seen from below.
The main force of the Red Army crossed from
the far side, where a rough track runs along
the bank.*

Pages 224-225: *Market street in the town of
Hanyuan, on the Dadu River south of Luding.
The slogan under the poster reads: 'Unite to fight
for success in modernisation and socialism'.*

HARALD SUND

义现代化建设的新局面而努力奋斗

KEN DUNCAN

KEN DUNCAN

★

Above: *Makeshift bridge in the foothills of the mountains beyond Luding.*

Left: *The meeting of two bridges between Tianquan and Baoxing, west of the Dadu River.*

★

Top: *Like hanging washing, drying noodles at Hanyuan, on the Dadu River.*

Above: *Lunchtime break amongst drying maize at Waguo village, south of Luding.*

Right: *The mountains and plateaux of west Sichuan province are areas traditionally inhabited by Tibetans. Many have mingled with the Han Chinese but they retain their customs and dress and their Buddhist beliefs. This woman lives in a village north of the Great Snowy Mountains. Tibetans fled in fear when the Red Army came through their villages, leaving no food for the hungry Communists.*

HARALD SUND

★

Left: *This woman of the Yi nationality lives in the village of Tianja, south of Luding. In this area the Yis were called Lolos by the Han Chinese, a name they found highly offensive. It was here that the Red Army sought the support of the Yis by giving them arms and ammunition and swearing blood brotherhood.*

Above: *Maize drying in the sun on Luding rooftops.*

Overleaf: *In towns and villages all over China people are now playing pool in the streets. Almost overnight it has become the most popular pastime. In Kangding even the local basketball pitch has been sacrificed for more pool tables.*

HARALD SUND

Building a cement works at Hanyuan, a small
town south of Luding. In the years following the
Long March, many homes were destroyed by
Japanese invasion and civil war. New housing
projects are still a priority today.

HARALD SUND

★

Men and women of the Yi nationality pose for a group portrait under the trees at Tianja village, south of Luding. The Yis are one of fifty-five minority groups in China, and of these, forty-eight are in the western provinces.

Right: *The Jiajin Mountain in the Great Snowy Mountains. The Red Army crossed by a pass at a height of fourteen thousand feet. Lack of oxygen killed the weak or wounded; men simply collapsed in the snow and died.*

Overleaf: *The approach to the Great Snowy Mountains between Baoxing and Lushan. The Red Army crossed in June 1935 as the weather deteriorated and thick snow and ice covered the higher passes.*

Pages 240-241: *Mount Dapao in the Great Snowy Mountains. During this part of the Long March the Red Army suffered losses from mountain sickness and lack of food.*

LEO MEIER

KEN DUNCAN

★

Many Red Army soldiers were surprised to find that so much of west Sichuan was peopled by Tibetans who had abandoned their villages, believing that Han Chinese troops had come to kill them and eat their children. Chinese government policy today is to encourage all minority peoples to preserve their national identity, as well as their arts and customs.

Far left: A Tibetan man at Garze, southwest of the Great Grasslands, where the Second and Fourth Front Armies linked up in July 1936.

Above left and left: Engraved belt ornaments worn by Tibetans.

Above: A Tibetan earring.

KEN DUNCAN

★

Above: *In this region the rivers are fast-flowing and extremely dangerous for ferryboats. One town may be many miles distant from its nearest neighbour, reached only by rough mountain tracks. A single suspension rope is often the only way to negotiate a river barrier.*

Right: *The way down from Jiajin Mountain in the Great Snowy Mountains. These wooden stakes in the cliffside are the remnants of the causeway used by men of the Red Army.*

KEN DUNCAN

LEO MEIER

★

Left: *Tibetan architecture at Garze, in the far west of Sichuan province. Tibetan houses are often very large, with the animals stabled on the ground floor, the living quarters above and a temple under the roof.*

Above: *Tibetan woman at Lazu village holding a Buddhist rosary.*

Overleaf: *View from a Buddhist temple at Garze. During the Cultural Revolution (1966-76), Buddhists came under attack and temples were destroyed. Now many of the monks have returned and temples have been restored.*

★

Top: Outdoor pool table in a Garze street. The cues are clumsy and the cloth rough but there is never a shortage of players.

Above: At Fubian village, not far from Garze, factories make bricks and tiles.

Right: View across the Garze fields to the grim mountain peaks beyond. Sixty miles west of Garze is Tibet, the roof of the world.

THE GRASSLANDS

OF ALL THE areas the Red Army passed through on the Long March, the Great Grasslands (known today as the Gannan Tibetan Autonomous Prefecture) has probably changed the least. The suffering of the soldiers here was particularly intense because they crossed at a time of bad weather when grassland had turned into treacherous marsh.

Today's inhabitants use the pastures to graze horses, yaks and sheep. Most are of Tibetan origin and their livestock provides their livelihood — milk and milk products, meat, hides and wool. The women spend much of their time weaving wool for tents, while the men generally stay with the herds. The inhabitants of the grasslands also grow barley, the staple grain. Nearly all are Buddhists. They wear colourful local dress and are excellent horsemen, enjoying several sports performed on horseback.

The Great Grasslands has obvious potential as a tourist area with the strange beauty of its landscapes, vistas of distant mountains, wealth of spring flowers and the warm friendliness of its people. Of particular interest to visitors is the beautifully decorated Tabrang Monastery, now re-established as a home for the monks and lamas who were driven away when the monastery was closed during the Cultural Revolution. At present, however, the area is inaccessible and lacks tourist facilities.

———————— ★ ————————

Left: *Near the town of Aba, at the western end of the Great Grasslands. The prayer flags on the roof of a house show it to be a holy place. A Tibetan lama is living here.*

Overleaf: *Work at a flour mill in Mao'ergai, on the southern fringe of the Great Grasslands. Buckwheat and barley were high in the fields when the Communists arrived in 1935 and they reaped a quick harvest.*

★

Left: A trader from near Heishui stares at the photographer through an amazing pair of antique handcrafted spectacles.

Above: A herdsman in Mao'ergai, the Tibetan equivalent of the Wild West cowboy.

Overleaf: One of the richest men in Aba performs an act of worship by lighting his yak butter lamps, which cost him the equivalent of seven US dollars a day. He owns two hotels, two shops and a transport team.

LEONG KA TAI

★

Above: *Tibetan woman milking. She belongs to a nomad family, living in tents and moving over the high plateaux with the herds.*

Right: *Farming near Mao'ergai. The same kind of plough has been used for centuries.*

LEONG KA TAI

———————————— ★ ————————————

Left: *A cowboy at Hongyuan (the word means Red Prairie), south of the Great Grasslands.*

Above: *Secondary school students at Hongyuan enjoy a Saturday night dance. The girls are Han Chinese. Tibetan cattlemen come in from the hills to watch the fun but do not dance.*

Overleaf: *By the time the troops of the Red Army reached this area of the Great Grasslands, near the town of Zoige, they had crossed the worst part and their seven-day ordeal was nearly over. Here the grasslands are free of marsh and swamp and provide rich pasture.*

Pages 266-267: *Monks in the lamasery at Aba, at the western end of the Great Grasslands. The number of acolytes is increasing and there are regular examinations on the Buddhist scriptures.*

LEONG KA TAI

★

Above: *This senior monk has an important part to play in examining the younger lamas in their knowledge of the holy scriptures. The examinations are a time of fun and laughter. Questions are shouted out by the lamas with a clapping of hands. If the answer is wrong, the examiner jumps for joy, before holding the examinee's head and shouting the correct answer in his ear.*

Right: *A well-known figure at the lamasery, this monk was the only member of the community to stay and receive the Red Army units when they passed through. Everyone else took flight.*

LEONG KA TAI

LEONG KA TAI

LEONG KA TAI

LEONG KA TAI

★

Left: *Tibetan prayer flags at Tanggor, in the middle of the Great Grasslands. The Tibetans of this region do not bury or cremate their dead but expose their bodies for the vultures or cast them into the River Gar. The prayer flags show that this is a holy place.*

Top and above: *A young villager at Tanggor meeting strangers from a distant country felt that something extra was required for a photograph. He decided on a clowning act.*

LEONG KA TAI

★

Left and above: *The Great Grasslands
between Tanggor and Zoige. This is the middle
stretch of swamp as the Red Army survivors
remembered it. They also suffered cold, wet mists
and rainstorms.*

★

North of the Great Grasslands the marsh and swamp give way to broad pastures where the Tibetans raise sheep and cattle as well as yaks. The whole area is around ten thousand feet above sea level. The Tibetans of the Great Grasslands honour the yak as the universal provider: they use yaks for transport and pulling ploughs; they drink yak milk and make rancid butter from it; they eat the yak meat and make ornaments from the long, curving horns; they use the hide and hair for clothing and material for tents. In the ice-covered heights of Tibet the yak is protected by a shaggy coat and long hair. Here in western Sichuan, when the warmer weather comes the yak loses its fierce and shaggy appearance and the pastures are bright with wild flowers.

Above: A young Tibetan girl milks a yak.

Above right: Herds of yak roam the flowering summer pastures.

Right: A small boy rounds up cattle at Zoige, north of the Great Grasslands.

Overleaf: A well-to-do Tibetan family in Aba assembled for lunch. The husband is dishing out yoghurt. At the back of the room is the 'kang', the raised part of the floor heated from below.

THE CAVES OF YAN'AN

NORTH SHAANXI, WHERE the Long March ended, is one of the poorer areas of China. Except in the valleys, good farming land is scarce. The soil is mostly loess — a yellow or chocolate-coloured earth covering thousands of square miles. There are several theories about how it developed: one suggests that it was carried by the wind from the far north; another that it was the mud of the sea-bed when northern China lay under the sea millions of years ago. The region was once covered with trees but now the forests are gone; when the rains come massive erosion occurs and tons of soil are washed away into the Yellow River.

The loess soil can be easily hollowed out to form cave dwellings, which are warm in winter and cool in summer. In the town of Yan'an, in the middle of the loess country, the Communists used cave houses as their homes and offices for ten years. Yan'an is officially regarded as the great historic centre of the Chinese Revolution. During China's war against Japan and in World War Two, it was the headquarters of the Red Army and the Chinese Communist Party.

Over the centuries Yan'an has seen many armies come and go, since Shaanxi province has been the invasion corridor from the north down into central China. The Great Wall, barrier against barbarians, runs across its northern sector.

Most of the people living in the area are farmers, but Yan'an itself is a thriving town of forty thousand inhabitants. The surrounding regions are being developed to exploit their rich coal and mineral reserves.

---------------------- ★ ----------------------

Scene near Yan'an, in Shaanxi province, where the Red Army, after completing the Long March, rested and gathered strength for the war against the Japanese.

LIU XIAO JUN

LIU XIAO JUN

★

Left: The last stages of the Long March lay through a part of Gansu province where many of the people were Muslims. Mounted Muslim bands supporting the enemy Guomindang harassed the tattered Communist columns as they pushed on towards journey's end. Today Muslims in China enjoy full religious freedom. This mosque is at Taohuashan, near Huining, where the First and Fourth Front Armies were united for the second time in October 1936.

Above: Worshippers in a mosque at Nanguan, near Minxian.

Overleaf: A local Chinese opera troupe which performs in the streets and markets of Shaanxi province. White make-up signifies the clown, although sometimes it stands for treachery.

Pages 284-285: The loess country near Huining, in Gansu province. Loess is a fine, light soil, yellow or chocolate-brown in colour, easily eroded by streams in the wet season, yet firm enough for caves to be dug. The Red Army lived in loess caves for years after the Long March was over.

At Yan'an a group of today's young Red
Army soldiers parade at the site of Mao's
old headquarters. They are holding a large
photograph of Mao and his officers taken
in 1936.

JEAN-PIERRE LAFFONT

Trading ponies at the market at Zhidan. This small town was called Bao'an when the Red Army settled here early in 1936.

★

General store at Wuqi, in Shaanxi province.
When the troops of the Red Army reached this
town they were almost at the end of their long
journey. Communist guides from the Shaanxi
soviet came out to meet them. Mao Zedong spent
three days in Wuqi before moving eastward.

JEAN-PIERRE LAFFONT

──────── ★ ────────

Above: *The cave house in Yan'an where Mao Zedong lived, now preserved as a museum. The museum keeper is in the far corner, his wife sits on the bed making shoes, and their child is on the floor near a family friend, preparing her lessons. These Yan'an cave houses are comfortable, though the windows are often covered with thin translucent paper instead of glass.*

Overleaf: *A field of buckwheat flowers near Lijiawan village on the road from Zhidan (formerly Bao'an) to Yan'an.*

Left: *The cave in which Mao Zedong lived in Zhidan (formerly Bao'an) from early 1936 until the following year.*

Overleaf: *The town of Wuqi, on the Luo River. A dusty, windswept region, it was once the poorest in China. Fifty years ago, Wuqi was a village with only seven families and one bachelor, who were often harassed by bandits. The village has grown into a town of four thousand people with schools, shops and electric light.*

Pages 296-297: *Cycle repairers along the side of a street in Yan'an. Since 1976, when the Cultural Revolution ended, small traders and repair shops have reappeared.*

JEAN-PIERRE LAFFONT

★

Left: *Fresh chillies drying in the sun in Chiaergo village, about three miles from Yan'an.*

Below: *A married couple in their cave home in the village of Chiaergo.*

Overleaf: *The pagoda at Yan'an, a famous landmark in the hills above the town. Mao Zedong and the Red Army moved into Yan'an in 1937 after the Long March and stayed until Guomindang troops threatened in March 1947. However, they continued to operate in northern Shaanxi until they were strong enough to seize the northeastern provinces and sweep south across China.*

THE MAKING OF THE LONG MARCH

The Story Behind the Project

★ First Steps

The Great Wall of China had never seen anything like it. Some of the world's finest photographers, their spirits high in anticipation of the adventure that was about to begin, were scrambling about the ancient stones like excited schoolchildren. They had come from all over the world for this assignment: from France, Italy, Switzerland, West Germany, the United Kingdom, Australia, New Zealand and the United States. Five were from the People's Republic of China itself.

The group portrait taken on the Great Wall on 31 August 1985 (see above) marked the starting point of one of the most remarkable

photographic operations ever undertaken — a section-by-section coverage of the route of the Long March made fifty years previously by the men who became founders of the People's Republic of China.

For the publishers, the project had already begun to assume an epic quality reminiscent of the Long March itself; so on that hot August morning in northern China it was gratifying to see that the big shoot was finally happening, exactly on schedule.

Nearly two years had passed since the idea of producing a book and a television documentary to commemorate the fiftieth anniversary of the Long March had been discussed. To do so by sending world-class photographers along the whole

length of the route was a daunting project — one that few, if any, other publishers would be willing to attempt. To do so as a joint venture with the Chinese publishing authorities was simply unprecedented.

Discussions with Mr Lou Ming, President of China National Publishing Industry Trading Corporation, revealed that the Chinese were interested in co-publishing a top-quality pictorial coverage of the march. Indeed, every publishing company in China planned to produce something on the subject. But this book was to be different: it would not only tell the world in words and pictures the story of the Long March itself but it would also provide an extraordinary portrait of China fifty years after the event.

With the decision made to pursue the idea, one of the first steps taken by the publishers was to seek the advice of Dr Stephen FitzGerald, former Australian ambassador to Beijing and a man highly respected by the Chinese authorities. Acting as special consultant to the project, FitzGerald helped sort out the numerous legal, financial, logistic and technical details before negotiating a contract with the Chinese co-publishers. This was signed on 23 January 1985.

Part of the agreement was that a survey team would make a reconnaissance of the six thousand-mile route prior to the big shoot which was scheduled for September 1985, when it was hoped that weather conditions would be most suitable.

Above: *The photographic team astride the Great Wall.*
From left to right, Jean-Pierre Laffont, Mary Ellen Mark, Michael Yamashita, Leo Meier, Adam Woolfitt, Paul Lau, Gregory Heisler, Mary-Dawn Earley (Project Director), Hans Verhufen, Yang Shaoming, Georg Gerster, Brian Brake, Leong Ka Tai, Harald Sund, Liu Xiao Jun, Zhang He Song, Di Xiang Hua, Wang Wen Lan, Enrico Ferorelli.

Left: *The photographers' photographer, Ken Duncan.*

★ Route Reconnaissance

The route reconnaissance from late April to early June 1985 was in many ways a rehearsal for the shoot that was to take place later in the year. The survey team gathered vital information about suitable photographic locations, transportation facilities and local weather conditions on the various sections of the route. Christopher Hooke and Leo Sullivan, two film-makers from the Sydney-based company, Independent Productions, joined the survey to obtain background footage before returning in September to film the photographers at work. Other members of the team included Wang Fayao, Director of the Trade Department of the co-publishers, China National Publishing Industry Trading Corporation; two interpreters, Li Dong and Qiao Hong; Swiss photographer, Leo Meier; and his Australian assistant, Harold Weldon, who was also the team's official diarist.

Weldon's diary of the journey contains fresh and vivid impressions of what it is like to be a Western newcomer to China; impressions that were to be verified by many of the photographers later in the year. He writes of almost continually being surrounded by crowds, especially in remote areas where the visit of a Westerner is a rare, if not unknown, event. Though the crowds were always friendly, they were often a hindrance to the photographers who wanted to record less contrived, more natural scenes. Weldon describes, too, the extraordinary friendliness of the people they met along the way, particularly in the rural areas, and of prodigious 'toastings' with liberal quantities of local liquor.

'Each street offers a book of photo opportunities,' Weldon writes of a market scene in Nanchang on 22 April. 'Hand-made fish-hooks, axe-heads, jewellery; a man frying fresh eels; a lady selling ice cream; old men playing cards; a woman washing underwear. Historical sites inspire, but here is real life. We are getting ever closer to today's China.' At Ruijin, a few days later, they met Red Army veterans, one of whom, Mr Gu Yuping, had been Zhou Enlai's personal bodyguard for the entire march. 'When Mr Gu proposed a toast at lunch and stood there with his glass raised we could sense his strength. The glass remained so steady, despite his age. His handshake hurt, it was so firm.'

Weldon's entry for 6 May in Kunming contains a typically Australian anecdote:

'Though a Swiss, Leo [Meier] has a

Harold Weldon's journal shows botanical specimens collected on the route reconnaissance and records the memorable meeting with Gu Yuping, who had been Zhou Enlai's bodyguard for the entire Long March.

passion for boomerangs. He has even been listed in the *Guinness Book of Records* for his prowess at throwing boomerangs. After lunch Leo desperately wanted to make a boomerang with some wood he'd bought. Li Dong discovered some hotel renovations were underway, so

Leo Meier with his home-made boomerang.

Leo borrowed tools from the workmen. Using a penknife he soon fashioned a boomerang. We raced off to the park to try a throw. It worked first time, the boomerang returning perfectly. Soon a crowd gathered and Leo let a couple of kids try it.'

The expedition wasn't all kids' play. At Jiaopingdu, Weldon writes:

'When we reached the climbing area I simply dissolved. Leo strode ahead while I stumbled along, gasping for breath. Even an old woman

donkey-tender passed me by. We reached a school where I found a room full of hay and flopped for rest. Schoolchildren accompanied us along the final leg back. A little girl to whom I'd given a kangaroo pin stayed back with me as I again struggled, breathless, up the path. We held hands and she led me along the way. My spirits lifted then.'

'At one stage,' the journal continues, 'we stepped over an old carved wooden and stone bridge into a forest glen that was Tolkien country. Mossy forest floor, old wiggly trees that could almost talk, little furry creatures scurrying among the trees and the constant babble of water. Magic!' Later the team made an assault on Jiajinshan, a peak in the Great Snowy Mountain range.

'After an hour's walk we reached the summit area. From here begins the true climb up, sloshing through soggy mud and small bushes up into the snow. The air was decidedly thinner above 12,500 feet and soon we reached the saddle of rock just below the peak. I pushed on up the steep rise to the summit. What glory on top! Our view stretched out to dozens of higher snowy peaks. Soaring above us was a huge bird of prey. All the hassles of organising this hike had become worth it. This was definitely the highlight of the trip.'

★ Countdown to the Shoot

As a result of information gathered on the route reconnaissance, two major decisions were made relating to the September shoot. First, it was apparent that several four-wheel-drive vehicles would be needed to cope with the rugged terrain in remote areas. Second, hot-air balloons would be invaluable for shooting low-level aerials. Both the Land Rovers and the balloons (plus crew and gas) would have to be brought into China from outside the country.

The scope of the project had now grown considerably and additional support was needed. The publishers

Mr Zhu Muzhi, former Minister of Culture, meeting the photographers in the Great Hall of the People.

approached a number of major companies, seeking financial and practical assistance. The response was gratifyingly prompt and generous. (For more on project sponsors, see page 318.) Five specially equipped Land Rovers and two hot-air balloons were shipped into Hong Kong. After completion of the required documentation, the convoy was driven into China through the border town of Shenzhen, centre of a Special Economic Zone recently established just north of Hong Kong.

By mid-July 1985, after months of planning, paperwork and further negotiations in Beijing, the stage was set. The photographic team had been selected (see pages 312—316) and it

was agreed that each member would be accompanied by an interpreter and a guide during his or her assignment. The Chinese publisher would attend to all visas, travel and accommodation arrangements internally, while the overseas publisher would handle all external matters. From the project office in Hong Kong, instructions regarding health precautions, clothing requirements, customs formalities, tickets and travel itineraries were dispatched to the photographers. The countdown had begun.

On 29 August the photographers began to arrive in Beijing. The next day, briefing dossiers were issued and each photographer was told which section of the route he (or in the case of Mary Ellen Mark, she) was to cover. Leo Meier raised everybody's

expectations with a slide show of the route reconnaissance.

That evening all members of the team attended an audience in the Great Hall of the People with Zhu Muzhi, then Minister of Culture, who had taken a personal interest in the project. This was followed by a banquet hosted by Mr Bian Chuen Guang, Director of China Bureau of Publishing Administration, and attended by a group of veterans from the Long March.

A wake-up call at 5.30 am on

31 August roused the team to buses waiting to take them to the Great Wall. As the buses pulled out of the Beijing suburbs into the countryside to the north of the city there was a symphony of clicking shutters and humming motor drives. Camaraderie between the Chinese and overseas photographers kept the interpreters busy with discussions on the photographers' inevitable topics of film and equipment.

A two-hour drive and brisk thirty-minute climb on the wall brought the team to the location for the group shot. Photographers spend their lives taking pictures of other people but when it comes to having their own photographs taken they can be very shy. The sense of this occasion, however, overcame all inhibitions. The 'long march' of the photographers was soon to begin.

By noon the team was back in the centre of the city at the famous old Beijing Hotel. Lunch was followed by a photography seminar in the magnificent ballroom. Brian Brake displayed an audiovisual study of his home country, New Zealand, while New Yorker Greg Heisler presented the quintessential photojournalist's slide tray. Swiss aerial photographer Georg Gerster treated the audience to a view of the world from above, a perspective that was entirely novel to many in the audience.

The day of departure, Monday, 2 September, when each photographer was to head for his assigned section of the route, began with an early morning audience in the Great Hall of the People. Madame Kang Keqing, widow of Marshal Zhu De, had requested to meet the team. Madame Kang, herself a veteran of the march, is alleged to have saved the lives of wounded soldiers by carrying them on her back. A powerful woman indeed! Today she is a leading figure in the Chinese government and a champion of women's rights. Madame Kang told the group that the most important task of her remaining years — she was then aged seventy-five — was to share the memories of her experiences during that incredibly difficult but ultimately triumphant struggle. Those memories, and the memories of the other veterans, were, of course, of vital interest to author Anthony Lawrence who was attending the audience, sitting in a place of honour near Madame Kang.

At noon the interpreters, all students at the Foreign Language Institute in Beijing, arrived to collect the first groups leaving on assignment. By five that afternoon the last had left. By plane, train, minibus, Land Rover, hot-air balloon, car, donkey and on foot, for the next ten days the photographers covered the six thousand miles of the Long March.

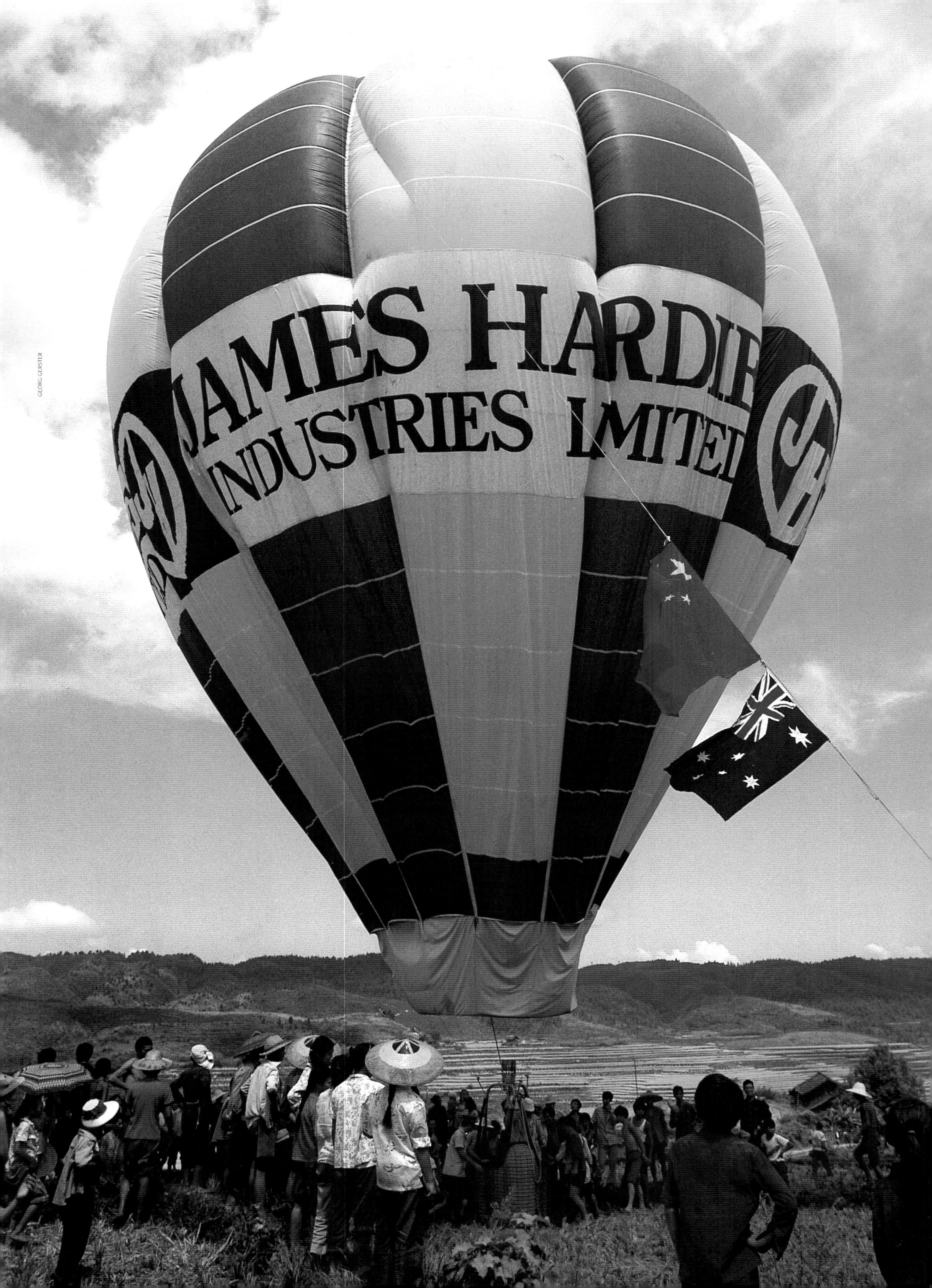

GEORG GERSTER

PETER VIZZARD

★ China by Balloon

It would be impossible to describe the separate adventures of all the photographers as they traversed the various sections of the route of the Long March: Leong Ka Tai's weird and wonderful encounters with Tibetan children; Ken Duncan's lonely climb to the top of a misty mountain where the photographic possibilities were zero; Paul Lau's daily assaults by rain; Jean-Pierre Laffont's trek through rivers of mud; or Hans Verhufen's intestinal problems which forced him to subsist on a diet of nothing but plain rice. Each photographer has a story about his own 'long march'.

Instead there follows an account of the most dramatic and colourful part of the assignment — the hot-air balloon adventure.

The reconnaissance had shown that the areas most suited to aerial photography were in the southern provinces of China, in Jiangxi, Hunan and Guizhou. As far as we knew, no one had ever photographed China from a hot-air balloon, so the logistical and administrative problems of the exercise were considerable. The Chinese co-publishers set about obtaining the necessary permissions. Meanwhile two balloons were shipped up from Australia to Hong Kong.

Weeks of nerve-wracking silence ensued until a flurry of telexes and exhortatory telephone calls produced the necessary permits. Four days later,

Left: *Early morning liftoff in Liping.*

Top: *In the basket, bespectacled pilot Peter Vizzard, camera-carrying Georg Gerster and interpreter Ma.*

Above: *Interpreter Li Dong and balloonists Judy Lynne and Peter Vizzard consult local maps.*

Overleaf: *The first balloon ascent at Ruijin attracted enormous crowds which surrounded the Land Rovers and support crew.*

GEORG GERSTER

the balloons were brought up to the mainland from Hong Kong.

The team included balloonists Peter Vizzard, 1983 world hot-air balloon champion, and Judy Lynne, 1984 Australian champion. A two-man film crew from Independent Productions, director Peter Butt and cameraman Stephen Arnold, were on board, as was Georg Gerster, widely regarded as the leading aerial photographer in the world. There were also drivers, interpreters and guides. Three specially modified Land Rovers transported the team, and included in the caravan was a large truck carrying two tons of propane gas supplied by Shell to fuel the balloons.

Eleven flights were made in the eight days required to cover the team's 932-mile route. Peter Vizzard did most of the flying, usually in the larger of the two balloons, with the second held in reserve. Judy Lynne directed the balloon retrieval team. As Vizzard recorded in his journal, crowds were a major concern:

'We kept wondering where they came from. One moment we were flying up the valley, with the world laid at our feet: a Chinese-style landscape with only the odd farmer in sight. The next moment, usually when we tried to land, there were wall-to-wall people below. On one occasion, we were forced to land in a rice paddy. The crowds were upon us before we could step out of the basket. We were seriously alarmed about the balloon

being trampled on as well as the poor farmer's crops being ruined.'

Another problem was finding adequate maps. The balloonists needed topographical details to inform them about the hills, valleys and rivers in the balloon's flight path. Persistent inquiries to the local authorities eventually met with success. A police escort arrived each morning carrying the map and returned each evening to take it back.

Photographer Georg Gerster had no problems; he was ecstatic throughout the trip. He enjoyed Vizzard's expert flying, good weather and superb vistas — the last especially so during the final stop in Zunyi. Gerster was in his element.

Balloon pilots and photographers are in total agreement about the best times of day to work: early morning and late afternoon produce the most favourable air currents for ballooning and the best light for photography. Judy Lynne recorded the events of the last day's flight:

'Awoke at five to the rustle of wind. All was ready by six: balloons, drivers, policemen and a local television crew. Wind quite strong on the way to launch site. Light rain was falling.

'Peter wanted to get away during a lull in the wind so we worked fast to inflate his balloon. It rocked and rolled on the ground. Georg was very excited at having an adventure. As the balloon launched it hit air turbulence and was severely buffeted about. Even Li Dong's [the interpreter's] eyes were wide as saucers as the balloon distorted out of shape. Peter climbed fast to get into a steadier windstream. Within seven minutes they had crossed the city and were entering the hills. Peter's last radio transmission: "Went straight over the city. Georg is beside himself with joy. Lost place on map. Headed on bearing of 340 degrees." And they disappeared.

'By 10 am we had not found them. At 10.30 I sent interpreter Ma back to the hotel in case a phone call came through. We drove about, stopping often to ask villagers, "Have you seen a balloon?" and finally at about noon we were on their trail. We left the road on a dirt track, drove as far as we could, and then started walking into a narrow valley with excited villagers leading the way. At 12.40 I spotted the basket surrounded by hundreds of people on a grassy knoll between paddy fields.

'Georg came to meet me, all excited, happy. He said he had got fabulous shots. They had flown only fifty minutes, but he said it was the best flight he had ever had. We returned to the hotel at two in the afternoon, very hot and very hungry. Peter and Georg were elated. I was completely exhausted!

'Georg's verdict on the adventure: "It was just like a holiday!"'

★ The Photographers

When word of the Long March project hit the professional grapevine, the publishers were deluged with telexes, letters and phone calls from photographers around the world. All carried the same plaintive message: 'Can I come too?'

Bearing in mind the nature of the assignments — arduous travel, work in remote areas, extremes of temperature and, despite the early reconnaissance of terrain, a number of imponderables — the publishers turned to photographers whose work included assignments for the American magazine, *National Geographic*. They had to be self-sufficient, produce the pictures, and return safely to base. Chinese participants were selected through the Chinese Photographers' Association, which experienced a similar rush of applicants from its eight thousand members.

Brian Brake
Country: New Zealand
Assignment: Hunan province from Anyuan to Daoxian

Recognised worldwide as a major photographic talent, Brake first won international acclaim when his 'Monsoon' photo-essay on India appeared in leading publications in 1961. A recipient of many important photographic awards, Brake received the Order of Merit from President Nasser of Egypt in 1969, and was made a member of the Order of the British Empire (OBE) by Queen Elizabeth II in 1981.

Brake had these reactions on this, his fourth visit to China: 'The friendship and co-operation given by our Chinese hosts have been overwhelming. They have taken me to locations of which I could only dream before, and into village situations I am sure few foreigners have seen. There has been no "dressing up" as there had been in the 1960s. I had complete freedom to photograph, an unbelievable freedom. Naturally, I would have liked more time — not just to record but in a small way to understand this "Chinese-ness". It would probably take forever.'

Di Xiang Hua
Country: China
Assignment: Sichuan province

Following his graduation from journalism studies at Beijing University in 1956, Di Xiang Hua taught photography for several years. In 1961, he began work as a photojournalist and is currently with *People's China*, a Japanese-language publication.

Di Xiang Hua drew the assignment to photograph in southwestern Sichuan province where there is a large population of colourful minority peoples. 'Everything was new to me,' he commented. 'In the Yi nationality autonomous region, I took many photos of Yi minority folk customs. It was an unforgettable experience.'

Ken Duncan
Country: Australia
Assignment: Sichuan province

Until four years ago, Ken Duncan was the senior technical representative of Pics Australia, a position he left in 1982 so that he might travel and work in central and northern Australia. He has continued to document remote areas of all that country's states and territories, paying special attention to the Australian Aborigines and their culture. The resultant book, entitled *Australia Wide*, is scheduled to be published in 1987.

Of his first visit to China, Duncan said: 'The Chinese are beautiful people. Many in my area are poor but what they have they are always willing to share. More than I can say for some of our well-off Westerners. The Chinese may be poor, but you rarely see an unhappy Chinese person.'

Enrico Ferorelli
Country: Italy
Assignment: Jiangxi province from Yongxin to Jinggangshan

Fluent in five languages and a qualified attorney, Ferorelli was attracted to photography in the late 1960s. In 1971, he decided to make his home in New York City, where he is in constant demand for assignments as diverse as a cover story on a famous artist for *Time* magazine and an essay on open-heart surgery for *Life* magazine. He was on assignment for that publication, working on a story about the King of Spain, when he was summoned to join the team in Beijing.

Of his first visit Ferorelli the linguist says: 'It was the most foreign

experience; not being able to read or understand felt strange. Normally you can always communicate. But it was all totally different from what I had expected. The old China has gone. Mao's China has gone. I loved it, and I was really happy in the countryside with the farmers. To me, that's the real China.'

Georg Gerster
Country: *Switzerland*
Assignment: *Jiangxi, Hunan and Guizhou provinces.*

For the past thirty years Gerster has contributed as a writer and photographer to *National Geographic* magazine, *Sunday Times* magazine, and *Paris Match*, among others, and his work has been featured in seventeen book titles. His speciality, aerial photography, was celebrated in the 1976 publication, *Grand Design, the Earth*

from Above. The recipient of nine major photography awards, Gerster has exhibited frequently over the past twenty years.

Recalling the trip, Gerster said: 'I had wanted to work in China for such a long time. It was like a dream come true. Everything was so well organised, and the people were so curious and friendly. I am used to working in airplanes. So the balloon was a special treat. It is such a stable platform, just beautiful and much closer to the ground than a plane. So we could see this fantastic landscape. Every inch of it used. Everywhere rice, rice.'

Gregory Heisler
Country: *United States of America*
Assignment: *Yunnan province*

Heisler, a native of Chicago now living in New York City, is in constant demand for editorial, corporate and

advertising assignments. Six years ago he completed his first cover stories for magazines such as *Life*, *Fortune*, *Esquire*, *Geo* and the *New York Times* magazine. His photographic essay on ballet dancers published in *Geo* magazine in 1982 resulted in a commission to shoot the entire American Ballet Theatre. The book, and a collection of large format studio dance portraits, were released the following year.

Of his time in China, Heisler says: 'The most striking thing about the people was that their curiosity about

me was as great as mine about them. Communication was no problem. You could sense the strong spirit in people and somehow instinctively understood them. It was utterly fascinating, but I felt frustrated seeing only people on the streets. I felt there must be more and so asked to meet a family in their home. Eventually, they arranged a visit with a well-known artist. He was very generous with the time he allowed for portraits with his two beautiful daughters. I also had a wonderful support team — my driver, in particular.'

Jean-Pierre Laffont
Country: *France*
Assignment: *Shaanxi province*

Based in New York and one of the world's busiest and best-known photo-journalists, Laffont covers news events in politics, science, economics and human interest topics. His assignment took him to the final section of the Long March, in Yan'an.

'Only half a day of sun, and tremendous crowds. I was the first Frenchman to visit Zhidan, so everywhere crowds. Very friendly but very curious. I had a young interpreter. I could not understand his English, but he could understand mine. He became a friend. My local guide was a photographer, he was a perfect person. He was very relaxed, and he understood *before* I spoke what I wanted to do. So I was very lucky. I loved every minute of this trip.'

Paul Lau
Country: Hong Kong
Assignment: Sichuan province

Self-taught, Paul Lau started taking photographs three years ago, many of them in China. The results of extensive travel within that country can be seen in the book entitled *China Unknown*, to which Lau was a major contributor.

Of his chance to work on this book Lau said: 'I was the youngest and least experienced photographer on the project, and I must say it was the most fantastic journey I have ever made in China. My assignment area was full of historical significance, but I was also aware of the changes over the past fifty years. It was a tremendous step in my career.'

Leong Ka Tai
Country: Hong Kong
Assignment: Sichuan — the Grasslands

Leong Ka Tai has worked as a professional photographer for the past nine years. He has travelled widely in China, and earlier this year published a book of his photographs on Beijing. He was especially pleased with an assignment that took him to the Grasslands:
'This trip held a double meaning for me. First I well knew the significance of the swamplands to the

Long Marchers, but I also have a fascination with the Yellow River. One of the high points of my travels was to see where the river looped through the three provinces of Qinghai, Gansu and Sichuan.'

Liu Xiao Jun
Country: China
Assignment: Gansu province

Liu Xiao Jun has been a photo-journalist with the China News Service since 1982. His work has appeared in both Chinese and overseas publications and he has won several photography awards in Beijing. He was a major contributor to the books,

Beautiful China, A Trip along the Yangtze and *Historical Relics of Three Kingdoms*.
'I was happy to meet the foreign photographers and make new friends. This was an important task, and I wish I'd had more time; especially so since it rained throughout the entire assignment period. It was a challenge which I hope was answered.'

Mary Ellen Mark
Country: United States of America
Assignment: Guizhou and Yunnan provinces

New Yorker Mary Ellen Mark's photographs have appeared regularly in most of the world's top publications over the past fifteen years, and she has also published several books. She is a regular on the photographic lecture circuit and has exhibited her work steadily since 1973. In the past few years she has been awarded seven of the most prestigious awards in photojournalism.

Though she spent long hours driving hazardous mountain roads and was plagued by bad weather, Mark has warm memories: 'I had a terrific interpreter: a lovely young woman who was so helpful and who really understood what I wanted to do. The food was great, the accommodation was very good and the people were so hospitable. What a great trip!'

Leo Meier
Country: Switzerland
Assignment: Sichuan province

Meier was trained in all aspects of printing and binding in Lucerne. In 1972 he emigrated to Australia, where he now resides. After his arrival in Sydney, he became a freelance photographer specialising in wilderness and wildlife. Four books of his photographs have been published and he has been a major contributor to many more.

Meier returned to the upper reaches of the Great Snowy Mountains for his assignment. Talking about the

Tibetan nomads he later recalled: 'It wasn't the brilliant colours of their clothes, nor the dazzling sparkle of their ornaments and jewellery that attracted me most; it was their smiles. No film could capture such feelings. I was completely disarmed.'

Harald Sund
Country: United States of America
Assignment: Sichuan province

Sund has been a professional photographer for seventeen years and his work has been featured regularly in leading magazines like *Life* and *Geo*, and in Time-Life books. He specialises in travel, landscape, nature, and corporate and industrial photography.

Included in his assignment areas were two famous sites of the Long March, Luding bridge and the town of Anshunchang, but it was the Tibetan plateau that captured his imagination: 'I never thought I would find a place, even a small remote area of the world, where I would be the first Western face

the natives had seen — but there it is, untouched, just as it has always been.'

Four months after his visit Sund wrote: 'I have reflected almost daily on this wonderful trip into the heart of China and have concluded that this is the most personally interesting assignment I have had in my professional career. It was a fabulous opportunity at the right time in China's history.'

Hans Verhufen
Country: West Germany
Assignment: Sichuan province — Jiaopingdu

Verhufen cared for the mentally handicapped until 1978, when he joined the staff of West Germany's best-selling magazine, *Horzu*. Following a year of illustration and design in the Art Department, he bought himself a Nikon camera and started working for

the German edition of *Geo* magazine. This led to assignments with other top publications and increased requests for work from German and American advertising agencies.

'From my reading on China, it was exactly as I expected. It was a tough assignment in that I am not used to climbing and walking. All that was entirely new. The Great Snowy Mountains reminded me of the Austrian Alps. I lost four kilos. I was most impressed by the farmers. Every last inch of the land was cultivated, no wasted space at all.'

Wang Wen Lan
Country: China
Assignment: Guizhou province from Liping to Jiangjiehe

Wang Wen Lan began his photographic career in the army, working for the PLA news report in 1974. Two years later he recorded the rescue efforts of the People's Liberation Army following the disastrous earthquake in Tang Shan city. Since 1981 Wang has worked as a

staff photographer for the *China Daily* newspaper. He is now director of the paper's Art and Photography group. Wang travelled through the Miaoling mountain area, steeped in the folk customs of the Miao minority peoples.

'When I was assigned to this project I was very excited, as the story of the Long March had left an indelible impression ever since my childhood. Recording the changes of the past fifty years, I experienced great feelings of confidence and hope for the future of my country.'

Adam Woolfitt
Country: England
Assignment: Hunan and Guangxi provinces

After working for a year on the staff of *Photography* magazine, Woolfitt began freelancing in 1961. He has worked for top publications throughout Europe

and the United States and has enjoyed an eighteen-year association with *National Geographic* magazine. To work in China had long been his goal. With a Land Rover at his disposal and perfect weather, he was not disappointed.

'My guides, drivers and interpreters were fantastic and we parted close to tears. Without them it wouldn't have happened like it did. I can't wait to get back to China and nothing will ever be quite the same again for me.'

Michael Yamashita
Country: United States of America
Assignment: Guizhou province from Guiyang to Loushanguan

Michael Yamashita studied Asian history at university and subsequently spent five years living and working in

Asia. Since 1975, he has specialised in photojournalism and travel photography, and has spent eight

years working for *National Geographic* magazine.

Yamashita, on his second visit to China, noted: 'The most impressive thing about my area [Zunyi] was the sense of history. It was the major turning point of the Long March and I was very conscious of it. But I was also impressed by the relative freedom I found, especially among the farmers. They work hard but are very friendly and appear happy. The trip was great, and it had a very emotional ending. My guide was almost in tears when I left.'

Yang Shaoming
Country: China
Assignment: Jiangxi province

A history graduate of Beijing University, Yang Shaoming was a keen amateur photographer for twenty years. In 1979 he decided to make

photography his career and joined the staff of Xinhua News Agency. He is a well-known photojournalist within China and published his first book on the Great Snowy Mountains and Grasslands in 1981.

As the son of two veterans of the Long March, his assignment in Jiangxi province held special significance. Following the shoot he wrote: 'I have accomplished the task in eleven days with intense emotion. I hope that you can use some of my pictures.'

Zhang He Song
Country: China
Assignment: Hunan province — Dayong, Sanzhi, Yinjiang

Zhang He Song has been shooting mostly sports photography with Xinhua News Agency since 1956. He has been official photographer on many mountaineering expeditions and is himself a certified second-grade professional mountaineer.

Quite at home in the mountainous border areas of Hunan, Guizhou, Sichuan and Hubei provinces, Zhang praised his country's progress: 'Fifty years ago Red Army soldiers climbed these mountains on foot and fought their enemies. We cannot imagine how hard it was. Today, every county has connecting roads, increased population and prosperity.'

Epilogue

By mid-September the photographers returned triumphant, some considerably slimmer than when they started. The film was shipped to Melbourne for processing and by early October the picture editing commenced.

From one hundred thousand images an initial 'rough edit' of nine hundred was selected. This selection was subsequently halved to create the final group considered for publication.

In early December, the Chinese co-publishers arrived to view the selection of photographs and review the historical text on the Long March. They pronounced themselves more than satisfied with what they saw.

The Mural

In January 1985 the publishers commissioned Chinese artist Zhao Zhun Wang to paint a mural on the theme of the Long March.

Preparations commenced in March 1985 when Zhao and his two assistants, Guo Shirui and Kang Le, travelled and researched the route of the march, making preliminary sketches and collecting reference material.

The mural, completed in January 1986, measures 60 ft by 6½ ft and was executed in Chinese ink and watercolours. It was presented to the people of China as part of the fiftieth anniversary celebrations. The artists accepted payment for materials but chose to contribute their talents to the project.

Born in Beijing in 1944, Zhao Zhun Wang studied first with the Chinese master painter Ya Ming at the Jangsu Painting Academy and subsequently with Cui Zi Fan in Beijing. In recent years he has completed murals in the Great Wall and Jianguo Hotels and the Beijing subway.

The mural of the Long March and its creator Zhao Zhun Wang.

Left: *The delegation from Beijing, from left, Lou Ming, Wang Hao, Deng Ligeng, with Project Director Mary-Dawn Earley and Editorial Director Elaine Russell.*

Above: *Picture editors, from left, Caroline Arden-Clarke, Mary-Dawn Earley and Zara Brierley.*

The Sponsors

CHINA: THE LONG MARCH could not have been produced without the support of its sponsors. A project of this magnitude, involving the co-ordination of the skills of so many people and the use of so much complex equipment and technology, depends on the help, goodwill and active sponsorship of many companies. To those listed below we offer our heartfelt thanks.

Kodak (Export Sales) Ltd

Growth and innovation have been hallmarks of the Kodak organisation for over a century.

Kodak began operations in China in the early 1900s and currently has liaison offices in Beijing, Guangzhou and Shanghai. China has always been an appreciative market for Kodak products, with a population eager to take advantage of the latest technology in photography, graphic arts, medicine, entertainment, business and education..

While pioneering ever newer and more sophisticated products, Kodak maintains its long tradition of meeting customers' expectations with quality products at affordable prices. The company is proud to know that its products continue to enhance the way of life in China.

Hutchison
HUTCHISON WHAMPOA LIMITED

Hutchison Whampoa Limited, which has had links with China for more than a century, is one of Hong Kong's largest and most successful investment holding and trading companies. With highly diversified business interests in property, container terminal operations, power generation, trading, retailing, quarrying and telecommunications, the Hutchison Group of companies is well positioned and committed to furthering trade relations with China.

C&L

Coopers & Lybrand's commitment in China dates back to early 1979 when Sanford Yung, founder of C & L Hong Kong, led a delegation of partners from C & L (International) to Beijing and effectively introduced the concept of management consultancy to the host country.

C & L is uniquely qualified to play a pivotal role in China's economic modernisation programme. The firm provides professional accounting, taxation and management consulting services in the People's Republic of China to foreign investors, local enterprises and government authorities, fulfilling at the same time a catalytic function in management technology transfer.

Coopers & Lybrand has representative offices in major Chinese cities including Beijing, Shanghai, Guangzhou and Shenzhen.

Cable and Wireless plc

Cable & Wireless' involvement in China's telecommunications spans just over a century.

The company currently has a joint shareholding and management role in two equity joint venture tele-communications service companies in Shenzhen SEZ, as well as being active in a number of other joint investment projects in Guangdong, Jiangsu and Zhejiang provinces. A recently conceived telecommunications-related scholarship scheme and a continuing programme of staff exchanges are two important features of the relationship. Through its subsidiary companies in Hong Kong and Macau, Cable & Wireless is also active in opening IDD telephone and other new services to an increasing number of destinations in southern and eastern China.

Companies of the Royal Dutch Shell Group have been active in China for many decades and in 1981 Shell China Limited was established with an office in Beijing to represent Shell in their activities in China.

These include oil exploration, trading and marketing of oil products, chemicals, coal, minerals and timber and the processing of Chinese crude oil.

In a number of areas Shell

Companies in Hong Kong have formed joint ventures with Chinese partners for the establishment and operation of oil storage depots, petrol stations and other facilities.

Over the past twenty years James Hardie Industries Limited, Australia's diversified trading and manufacturing group, has developed exports for China in materials used in tanning, food processing and pharmaceuticals. James Hardie has assisted in the manufacture and marketing of China's jute cloth, and in the development of new agricultural irrigation projects enabling China to grow subtropical fruit and vegetables for its expanding tourist market. Hardie's commitment to China also includes the sponsorship of visits to Australia for Chinese teachers.

Land Rover Limited supplied five of its latest One Ten and Ninety series Land Rovers for use in the Long March project. These vehicles were specially designed for the arduous conditions they experienced in China, with winches, roof racks and raised air intakes. In fact, they were capable of going anywhere.

The company saw the Long March project as yet another way of demonstrating the enormous strength and versatility of its vehicles to the world.

A strong commitment to China's development and emergence as a major travel destination parallels Holiday Inn International Asia/Pacific's development plans for the rest of the region. Holiday Inn Lido Beijing, the chain's first hotel in China, marks the beginning of an exciting era of expansion, including plans for hotels in

Xiamen, Guangzhou, Guilin, Shanghai, Shenzhen and Xian.

Ansett.

Ansett and the word aviation are synonymous to Australians. Ansett and its associated airlines developed in the pioneering era of commercial aviation. It has a large and modern jet fleet and a long association with aviation development in the Pacific area. Ansett has developed the experience, strength and systems to assess and take swift advantage of aviation development throughout the world. It recently established a worldwide aviation company to make its skills and a separate fleet of jet airliners available to airlines and governments throughout the world. Ansett is developing joint ventures with China.

PANALPINA
5 Continents – 1 Forwarder

The Swiss Panalpina Group, a leader in the worldwide shipping and forwarding business, is progressively strengthening its position in China. In close co-operation with the Chinese State Corporation, Sinotrans, various transport agreements have been concluded for which Panalpina is the responsible agent. Offices have been opened in Beijing, Shanghai and Guangzhou to facilitate services and to underline Panalpina's total commitment to China's future development.

HILL AND KNOWLTON

In 1984, Hill and Knowlton became the only international public relations firm to provide a complete service operation on-site in China, enabling major multinational corporations to conduct total communications programmes in one of the world's most challenging markets and offering local public relations counsel to Chinese organisations doing business overseas.

Hill and Knowlton, Beijing, is backed by a global network of offices providing media, corporate, financial and government relations counsel as well as full support services.

Index

Note: Picture references are indicated in italics.

Acknowledgments

The publishers would like to thank the following people for their help in the preparation of this book:

Bryan Anstee • Stephen Arnold • Mike Bailey • Nick Bailey • Louise Baldwin • Bao Yiming • John Bartley • David Bonavia • Michael Brierley • Mervyn Butcher • Peter Butt • Woodfin Camp • Zelda Cawthorne • Jean-Marc Charpenet • Mason Chan • Clement Chan • Gaylord Chan • Stella Chan • Chang Zhenguo • Chen Hairuo • C.C. Cheng • Edmund Cheung • Law Wai Cheung • Wendy Cheung • Cecilia Choi • Peter Cook • Pat Corrigan • Ron Cromie • Dai Yuyuan • Jan Davis • Ding Jianyi • Dong Yibing • Du Pingfa • Du Xudong • Sue Earle • Stephen Ellis • Terence Fane-Saunders • X.C. Fok • Graham Ford • Gao Mingguang • Paul Giannotis • John Guy • Diana Haigh • William Hall • Hao Gongliang • Chris Hilton • Chris Hooke • John Howard • Mike Howard • Hu Junhai • Graham Hurrell • Dee Huxley • Ken James • Jiang Guihua • Jin Shiyuan • Jim Kelso • See Foon Koppen • Ben Kwan • Helen Kwok • Kenneth Kwok • Ronnie Lau • Esther Lau • Samuel Lau • Irmgard Lawrence • Tommy Lee • Brian Leung • Anthony Leung • Li Lansun • Li Qi • Tony van der Linden • Paula Litsky • Liu Jiayu • Long Wenshan • Dawn Low • Luo Yuanhong • Luo Zhonghai • Derek Lygo • Miss Man • Vincent Mang • Kay Marles • John McFadden • David Macfarlane • Irene Meier • Miao Jinzhu • A.I. Morley-Fletcher • Simon Murray • Peter Ng • Dominique Nordmann • Okimitsu Ohishi • Shigeki Ohyama • Warren Penney • Clement Poon • Francis Poon • Taco Proper • Klaus Riebesehl • Sally Rodwell • Geoffrey Roper • Eleanor Sackett • Pam Seaborn • Gene Scott • Lionel Seah • Todd Sharvell • Brian Shell • Shen Zaiwang • Kevin Sinclair • John Slaughter • Jack Spackman • Joe Spitzer • Leo Sullivan • Sun Bin • Richard Sun • Ted Thomas • Amelia Thorpe • Tong Kuan • David Tress • Vivian Tse • Arnie Tucker • Mike Venables • Wang Hairu • Wang Pinsan • Julia Wilkinson • Roderick Wilson • C. Windfuhr • Laurie Winfrey • Anita Wong • K.H. Wong • Wu Fuan • Yang Xinshu • Cecilia Yeung • Yin Zeyao • Nelphen Yung • Sanford Yung • Zhai Yiwo • Zhang Binggao • Zhang Huiying • Zhang Jiaqi • Zhao Shijiang • Zhou Jiyao • Zhou Shuiyi • Ernst Zimmerman • Zu Yingnan •